RORY MOULTON

53 Amsterdam Travel Tips

Secrets, Advice & Insight for the Perfect Amsterdam Trip

First edition

ISBN: 978-1-7286657-8-8

This book was professionally typeset on Reedsy.
Find out more at reedsy.com

Contents

II   Go >> See >> Do

III   Indulge

FREE Paris eBook

Receive a FREE Paris ebook today.

After downloading your free book, you'll receive a monthly VIP email with book giveaways, new book announcements and huge book discounts ONLY available exclusively to subscribers.

Join the crew and subscribe for **FREE** to Rory Moulton's monthly email newsletter about European travel, "*EuroExperto*." In addition to the giveaways and discounts, receive the month's best European travel articles, news, tips, trends and more. I'll never spam you. I don't do ads. And you can unsubscribe at any time.

Smarter European travel is just a click away:

www.rorymoulton.com

Also by Rory Moulton

Other works available from the author:
- 53 Paris Travel Tips
- Paris with Kids
- Washington, DC with Kids
- 99 Things To Do in Paris with Kids

Introduction

Originally founded as a humble, swampy fishing town, Amsterdam grew into the world's premier trading center during the 17th-century Dutch Golden Age. Although the Dutch capital is no longer the epicenter of global trade, it remains one of the most-visited capitals in Europe. Drawing millions of visitors a year, Amsterdam rakes in international and European tourists. For 'Dam good reason, too. Amsterdam has it all: Museums. Restaurants. Bars. Breweries. Clubs. Pot shops. Cozy cafes. Outdoor markets. Huge parks. And those oh-so-picturesque canals.

But there's much more to Amsterdam than sightseeing, eating and partying. This is a city with a famed tolerance of diverse lifestyles and a social contract founded on acceptance. For religious "heretics" in the Reformation Period, Amsterdam meant freedom to worship. For homosexuals in the repressed 1950s until today, Amsterdam stands for freedom to love. For artists and creatives, Amsterdam offers unencumbered freedom of expression. And, yes, for pot heads, Amsterdam represents freedom to smoke. How can one city handle so much freedom? And it's not even in America...

Then there's the bewildering resilience of this city and its clever people. Built upon reclaimed land and constantly battling back the ever-encroaching North Sea, Amsterdam somehow balances the world's most-advanced technology with a reverence for the past. And to top it all off, no people in the world better appreciate and enjoy every day with such gusto as the Dutch.

From humble fishing town to international beacon of free- dom, Amsterdam continues growing and changing, charting a unique, innovative path forward that must be experienced to be understood. Without question, Amsterdam is one of my favorite cities not just in Europe but anywhere in the world. I hope you'll see that shine through in 53 Amsterdam Travel Tips.

I

Survive & Thrive

Essential and practical information for Amsterdam travel.

1

Learn a Little Dutch

And I do mean a little because, while that little bit of Dutch you're about to learn will come in handy once or twice, it's primarily a polite gesture. You see, most Dutch, especially Amsterdam's cosmopolitan urbanites, speak better English than you. And me (Or, is it *'and I'*...?)

Regardless, a savvy traveler learns at least a handful of greetings and phrases, if for no other reason than it's good ground-level diplomacy. Remember, when you travel you represent your countrymen (for better or worse). And there's no better diplomat than a respectful and intellectually curious traveler. So, Mr./Ms./Mrs. Ambassador, practice and memorize these pleasantries and you may even illicit a forced smile from the famously reserved Dutch:

- **Hello** :: Hallo :: *"HAH low"*
- **Good morning** :: Goedemorgen :: *"KHOO duh MORE khen"*
- **Good afternoon** :: Goedemiddag :: *"KHOO duh midakh"*
- **Good evening** :: Goedenavond :: *"KHOO dun AH fohnt"*
- **Goodbye** :: Dag :: *"d*akh*"*
- **Thanks** :: Bedankt :: *"b*uh DAHNKT*"* (informal)

3

- **Thank you very much** :: Dank u wel :: *"dahnk oo vel"* (formal)
- **Please/If you please/You're Welcome** :: Alstublieft :: *"ALST oo bleeft"* (formal)
- **Please/If you please/You're Welcome** :: Alsjeblieft :: *"ALS yuh bleeft"* (informal)
- **Excuse me** :: Pardon :: *"par DOHN"*
- **Mister** :: Meneer :: *"muh NEAR"*
- **Ms/Miss/Mrs** :: Mevrouw :: *"muh FROW"*
- **Sorry** :: Sorry (just like in English!)
- **Check, please** :: Te rekening, gelieve :: *"De rekening alstublieft"* (informal)
- **I'd like a beer.** :: Ik wil graag een biertje :: *"Ik vil khrahkh ən BEERtyə."*
- **I'd like a bottle of water.** :: Ik wil graag een fles water. :: *"Ik vil khrahkh ən fles VAtər."*
- **I'd like a order of fries.** :: Ik wil graag een portie friet. :: *"Ik vil khrahkh ən POORtsee freet."*
- **May I have a ...?** :: Mag ik een ...? :: *"Makh ik ən"*

2

When to Go

Before setting a departure date, let's run through what you can expect from Amsterdam's weather and tourism seasons.

Is there ever a "good" weather time?

Amsterdam is famous for a lot of things, but sunny weather isn't one of them. While summer indeed brings some gorgeous sunny days, most of the year Amsterdam rains at least once every two days. It's rare for temperatures in the summertime to go any higher than 75 degrees Fahrenheit.

Despite iconic images of ice skating frozen canals seared into our collective mind, temperatures nowadays don't stay below freezing for very long, even in the winter season. But since Amsterdam is below sea level it's often very foggy and bone-chillingly damp. Anyone visiting in the wintertime is advised to pack sweaters, scarves, hats, gloves and a waterproof coat.

Temperatures in the months of May and September are ideal because they tend to hover between lows of 50 and 65 degrees

Fahrenheit. Another bonus of visiting in the springtime is that the famous Amsterdam tulips reach full bloom.

The highs and lows of travel Amsterdam season

Unsurprisingly, Amsterdam's tourist traffic peaks come July and August. Anyone planning a visit in the jam-packed summer season should expect a crowded old city center, long wait times at popular attractions and higher prices at all restaurants, bars and hotels.

If you're only looking for a bargain, then consider visiting over winter, weather be damned. Flights into Amsterdam and hotel prices drop dramatically during this dark and rather dreary time of year. Just be forewarned, temps in December through February range between 32 and 41 degrees Fahrenheit and days with ample sunshine grow scarce. On the other hand, that's ideal museum weather.

The two top months to visit Amsterdam:

In my opinion, the best time to visit Amsterdam is either in May or September. Not only will you experience milder temperatures and less rain during these months, you'll also encounter far fewer tourists. And Amsterdam's clubs, restaurants and hotels won't jack up prices. Plus, you're more likely to discover opportunities to chat with locals before and after the annual tourist onslaught.

3

Schiphol Alternatives

Flights to Amsterdam's main airport, Schiphol, can be expensive or inconvenient based on your overall travel plans. Therefore, always compare rates with a few cheap airports nearby and other big European airports with direct rail connection to Amsterdam, like Paris and Frankfurt. And always hunt bargain Scandinavian carriers like IcelandAir, WOW Air and Norwegian.

While you'll find major airports easily, also consider my list of lesser-known Schiphol Airport alternatives below. Certainly, all of these cities themselves merit a night or two of your time — should your itinerary permit.

1. Düsseldorf International Airport (DUS)

Due to a huge international business community, direct flights into Düsseldorf can be found for shockingly cheap from North America and Asia. A direct train line whisks you from the airport to Amsterdam Centraal Station for as low as €19 each way. Make sure you book your rail tickets 60-90 days in advance and check for promotional fares.

2. Brussels International (BRU)

This airport used to require a train connection in Brussels, but since has made Amsterdam travel easier with a direct train from BRU to Amsterdam costing only about €39 each way. Again, crazy-cheap fairs from North America into Brussels pop up all the time.

3. Rotterdam Airport (RTM)

A third cost-effective option for flying to Amsterdam is Rotterdam. A high-speed rail connection delivers you straight into Amsterdam in about 40 minutes. Rotterdam is particularly appealing when flying within Europe since multiple budget carriers fly here.

4

Five Killer Apps

D on't staying buried in your phone when exploring Amsterdam. But checking a handful of key apps will make the trip run smoother and more enjoyably. General travel apps abound, but I suggest keeping it lightweight with:

- **Google Translate**
- **Google Maps**
- **Kindle/ebook reader app**
- **TripIt**

That's about it. Save plenty of storage space for photos, videos and these five killer apps designed specifically for Amsterdam:

1. Rijksmuseum app

The "Rijks," following the lead of other monstrous European art museums like Paris' Louvre, released their own in-house mobile app. And just like those others, it's a revelation. Experience more with extra info of the art (including a cool zoom feature), guided tours and a ticket-booking engine from which you can scan your tickets at the door.

iTunes + Android

2. 9292

This handy app helps you find your way around Amsterdam and beyond, providing public transport advice for the whole of the Netherlands, including all major public transport operators and the national railway network. Everything's integrated and updated in real time. Yes, there is certainly functionality overlap with Google Maps. Yet, I still find myself opening this app every trip to confirm routes or search for a new one.

iTunes + Android

3. Iamsterdam Maps & Routes

This app could use a better name — it's more a walking map/neighborhood scavenger hunt. However, I've really enjoyed exploring Amsterdam's neighborhoods using this app as my guide. I've gone places I wouldn't have gone and learned facts I wouldn't otherwise know. Additionally, it has pointed me in the right direction of some bars and restaurants I now consider favorites. I haven't utilized the gaming aspect — you can win prizes and unlock secrets — but I consider that gravy atop an otherwise solid app.

iTunes + Android

4. Amsterdam Travel Guide and Offline City Map

This German company produces a range of high-quality European city maps. Okay, yes, again some overlap exists with Google Maps. But editorial curation and a slick offline interface makes this travel guide a keeper. Of all the maps/guides available in app stores, this one — and indeed all the guide apps from Ulmon — stands above the rest.

iTunes + Android

5. FlatTire - Mobile Bicycle Service: Fix it!

So, you rented a bike. Then you got a flat tire. Now what? Well, good news. There's an app for that. Available from Mon-Sun 9AM to 9PM, this mobile-based bike repair service allows you to schedule a time and set your location. They'll name a price and then come to you, toolbox in-hand.

iTunes + Android

5

Am I in the Netherlands or Holland?

Trick question: You're in both! Consider this: You can visit the Netherlands without setting foot in Holland, but you can't visit Holland without being in the Netherlands.

Let me explain: Amsterdam resides within "Holland," which is a regional name covering two administrative provinces — North Holland (Amsterdam) and South Holland (Rotterdam and The Hague). It's like referring to the northeast United States as New England; there is no political entity called New England, but Americans know the term means a collection of states in the country's northeast.

The Netherlands — technically, the "Kingdom of the Netherlands," — is the official name for the whole country, which comprises 12 total provinces, including North and South Holland plus 10 others. Holland is home to the country's largest population bases, not to mention its greatest economic and cultural contributors. Therefore, the name Holland has been commonly and inaccurately applied to the whole country since Napoleonic times.

There you have it: Amsterdam is the city. Holland is the region. Netherlands is the country. Moving on!

6

#TramLife

Getting around Amsterdam primarily means riding trams, pedaling bicycles and walking. After bicycles, which we cover in another chapter, trams are Amsterdam's transportation lifeblood. Let's start learning how to get around Amsterdam with a look at the city's ubiquitous tram system. Ready for #TramLife?

Trams are safe, clean, ultra-punctual and easy to navigate. Even though locals prefer bicycles, I recommend travelers start out exploring Amsterdam by tram first. In fact, you may never feel brave enough for biking, in which case the tram and foot-power will surely provide all the connectivity you'll need to see Amsterdam. All of it. Guaranteed.

Amsterdam trams are quite distinctive. They are blue and white in color and their well-known bell rings to warn approaching cyclists and pedestrians. From Centraal Station to the neighborhoods around it, the tram is one of the quickest ways to get around and into the city center.

There are two tram stations outside the front of Centraal Station — one on the east side and one on the west. These stations are only a short distance from each other. There are 16 tram routes, 10 of which (lines 1, 2, 4, 5, 9, 13, 16, 17, 24 and 26) begin and end at Centraal Station.

One-hour, 24-hour and 48-hour tram tickets are available. Buy a 24-hour card when riding three times or more in 24 hours. Do some back-of-the-envelope math to decide if the other cards will pull their weight. Don't forget to bring a credit card since Amsterdam trams no longer accept cash payment. The Iamsterdam City Card (chapter 19) not only gives cardholders free entry to the city's top attractions, it also provides unlimited free public transportation. Hardcore sightseers, take note.

Trams have one access door that opens automatically, normally toward the rear; arrowed indicators point the way to the door. To board a tram that has no arrowed indicators, push the button beside the door on the outside of any car. To get off, you may need to push a button with an "open-door" graphic or the words "*deur open.*" Tram doors close automatically, and they do so quite quickly, so don't hang around. Always remember to hold your transit card against the reader as you get on and off the tram, aka "Don't forget to check out," a phrase you'll hear repeatedly on your tram journeys.

For a wonderful interactive map with which you can toggle on/off all tram routes, go to the GVB website here.

7

Who Will Save Your Soles?

Walking Amsterdam is lovely...for a day or two. After that, your dogs will bark and your thoughts will turn to renting bikes. Riding the trams is also lovely and relaxing (usually). But you'll grow envious of all those happy people on bikes, especially on a nice day. Again, you'll start to eye renting a bike.

And you should! But before you do, here are some helpful guidelines and tips to build your confidence for what is surely one of Europe's most-chaotic urban biking scenes.

First, if you're not used to biking in busy downtown traffic you'll be a bundle of nerves by the end of the trip. Venture across the river IJ into Amsterdam Noord (north) instead. Take the free ferry ride at the IJ-side of Central Station (i.e., the side *not* facing downtown). Visit NDSM, a former ship wharf (once the largest in the world) that currently is a 'breeding place' for artists and chefs. Or take the IJplein ferry and head for Schellingwoude, a lovely small village at the Oranje locks. Another easygoing option is to ride the bike path east to Haarlem.

But eventually, you'll return to Amsterdam proper. Therefore, keep in mind three tips:

- Always lock your bike. Always.
- Use the bell. Know it. Love it. Ring your bell to warn pedestrians, pass other bikers and alert oncoming vehicles.
- Mind the canals. After an Amstel and a puff they can appear seemingly out of nowhere. Exercise caution crossing bridges over canals. I once asked someone how deep the canals are. His reply, "About one meter of water and three meters of bicycles." He wasn't joking. 12-15,000 bikes are fished from canals annually. Don't let yours be one of them.
- Follow and obey all traffic lights. Bikers start and stop separately from vehicle and pedestrian traffic.

8

Other Means of Transport

Buses

After trams, taking buses makes the most sense for travelers. Unlike trams that have an entrance in the front, middle and back, Amsterdam buses only have a front entrance. If you get on the bus in the middle or back doors, you will run into angry people trying to get off the bus. The bus driver will also publicly shame you over the speaker. So, get on in the front.

During the day, rates run €2.80 for an hour-long trip, paid only by credit or debit card. This bus fare includes one transfer to tram, another bus or metro. If you are still on the bus after an hour, you'll be forced to buy another ticket. If you plan to travel by bus on a regular basis, you can buy a one-day, two-day or up to one week of bus fare at one time. Nighttime bus fares jump to €4.50/hour.

Just like the tram, buses have a public transport chip card that you have to show when you get on and off public transportation.

You put your card on the gray OV-Chipkaart electronic pad until it beeps, flashes a green light and informs you, "*Goede Reis.*"

Exit the bus through the middle or back doors and, as always, don't forget to scan your ticket on the way out.

Metro

Amsterdam has a growing metro system with five lines. They run partly over ground to transport commuters in and out of the suburbs, from 6AM to midnight every day. From Centraal Station, you can hop a metro train to both Nieuwmarkt and Waterlooplein in the old city center.

Pedicabs/rickshaws

If you believe in getting around town the environmentally friendly yet also lazy way, then a pedicab/rickshaw is the method of transportation for you. They are clean, rather cozy and easily weave through the cobbled streets of Amsterdam. They are also fully insured, fyi. You can find one easily throughout town, especially near Centraal Station, Leidseplein, Museumplein and Waterlooplein. Rates start at €30 per ½ mile.

Ferries

Three free ferries depart from the north side of Centraal station. (Yes, you can take your bike with you.) Ferries are an ideal way to catch beautiful views of the harbor and explore northern Amsterdam on the opposite bank of the IJ River, a place few travelers venture. These ferry routes are discussed in greater detail in later chapters.

Taxis

You can hail a taxi off the street or find a taxi stand at places like luxury hotels and major public squares. They have signs on their roofs and blue license plates. If you are staying in a hotel, the hotel staff can call a cab for you. Taxis are cost-effective for groups of 3 or more, especially at night when tram rates double.

Rental cars

Don't even bother. Amsterdam lacks ample parking spaces and roads can be terrifying to navigate for newbies. Therefore, if you arrive by car, it is a good idea to return your rental or park it long-term outside the city center. In the suburbs, there are plenty of park-and-ride options charging about €8 for 24 hours. From these, you can ride a tram or metro into the city.

9

This Kruidvat Deal is All That

G enerally speaking, you won't find a lot of deals or discounts on travel passes in Amsterdam. But one deal to keep an eye out for is the discounted ride-all-day train ticket occasionally offered by the Dutch pharmacy chain, Kruidvat.

The deal

Several times a year, Kruidvat offers its ride-all-day *Trein Dagkaart* (train day ticket) which allows unlimited travel for one person for a day on the entire Dutch rail network. Once in use, the ticket will automatically expire at 4AM the following day.

How to best use it

Day trips from Amsterdam. That's the key. The best use of these tickets is to take long day trips and/or make multiple stopovers during your travel day. Head out to some outlying Dutch cities such as Maastricht, Middelburg or Groningen. Examples are:

- Amsterdam-Maastricht-Valkenburg, with possible stopovers in Utrecht, Den Bosch, Eindhoven or Roermond.
- Amsterdam-Groningen-Leeuwarden and on to the Friesian coastal villages of Hindeloopen and Stavoren.
- Amsterdam-Middelberg/Vlissingen with stops in Breda, Dordrecht, Rotterdam etc.

Logistics

Buy your tickets at any Kruidvat outlet or online (you can request free pickup at any Kruidvat store). Costing just €15.99 (or €14.99 each for 2 tickets; €13.99 each for 3+ tickets), it is valid for a period of 2 months. For reference, a standard off-peak Holland Travel Ticket valid all day costs €39, so the Kruidvat ticket cuts your cost by more than half. It's a steal if you can score one.

If you're traveling with children 4-11, skip the Kruidvat deal and purchase a standard Rail Runner ticket at the station for €2.50, which is also valid the whole day. Children aged 0-3 travel free on the Dutch rail network. The Kruidvat pharmacy chain operates 29 stores in the Amsterdam area, including these tourist-friendly locations:

- Nieuwendijk 160 (near Dam Square)
- Kalverstraat 226 (near Muntplein)
- Regulierbreestraat 22 (near Muntplein/Rembrandtplein)
- Jodenbreestraat 96B (near Waterlooplein)
- Bilderdijkstraat 73-87 (west Amsterdam)
- Kinkerstraat 244 (west Amsterdam)
- Van Limburg-Stirumstraat 58 (Westerpark area)
- Jan Van Galenstraat 114h (west Amsterdam)

- Ferdinand Bolstraat 33-39 (de Pijp)
- Ferdinand Bolstraat 125-127 (de Pijp)
- van Woustraat 98-102 (de Pijp)
- Dapperplein 62 (east Amsterdam)
- Rijnstraat 53-55-57 (Rivierenbuurt)
- Maasstraat 46-48 (Rivierenbuurt)
- Oostelijke Handelskade 1033 (KNSM island)

10

Never Get Lost

While small and compact, Amsterdam's layout causes frequent bewilderment. Therefore, I wrote this chapter to narrate the city's design, noting its key neighborhoods and landmarks. And, of course, the canals. Of which there are 165 in Amsterdam. I expect you to learn all of their names. There will be a test.

But seriously, grab a city map or dial up Google Maps while reading this chapter and you'll never get lost. At least not in Amsterdam!

Downtown

The old center is very beautiful but also very much an open-air museum heaving with tourist traffic. Due to the semi-circular shape of the city you'll never be far from downtown, so you can dip in and out easily as your tourist-horde tolerance ebbs and flows.

The downtown hub — Centraal Station — anchors the old city's northern edge along the IJ River. Upon arrival, you'll likely stumble out into the Stationsplein, home to a dizzying array of trams, cars, bicyclists and buses. The old city center is just a block away, but exercise caution crossing these busy streets. Behind Centraal Station, the River IJ connects Amsterdam to the North Sea and buffers the trendy neighborhoods to the north from the bustling tourist zone.

The main canals — Singel, Herengracht, Keizersgracht and Prinsengracht — form a semi-circle around the old city center. Walking from downtown, you'll cross these four canals to reach the outer neighborhoods, including the much-recommended De Pijp and Jordaan areas. As beautiful (and heavily touristed) as they are, some smaller canals on the east side of downtown are actually older and have at least as much character. And nary a camera-wielding tourist in sight.

The 'Hoods

The neighborhoods below are described as a half circle starting west of downtown, going counterclockwise from west to south to east.

West and southwest of the center there's a lot of action these days. The Westerdok (Western Docklands) has been transformed into upscale residential zones. A bit further out west, beyond the excellent Westerpark and still on the water, is the Houthavens area, which is currently being redeveloped.

Immediately to the south of the Westergasfabriek area is the Staatsliedenbuurt, which used to be a no-go area in the 80s with squatters and a fierce independent, anarchist streak. Thankfully, it's much more welcoming now, but still less gentrified than other "formerly rough" areas in the midst of redevelopment.

Further South is the Kinkerbuurt where you'll find the rec-ommended Foodhallen / De Hallen complex (chapter 43) . Continuing further south, you end up in the Vondelpark area, surrounded by 100-year-old mansions and Amsterdam's posh-est neighborhood (Oud Zuid). Museumplein sits prominently nearby, home to the Rijksmuseum (Dutch masters), Stedelijk (modern art) and Van Gogh museums, as well as most of the tourists who aren't in the old center.

Going east from Vondelpark you'll get to De Pijp (chapter 12). This is hipster central with some admittedly overhyped and pretentious places, but still my favorite overall neighborhood and frequently my home base when I'm in Amsterdam.

Cross the beautiful Amstel River that lent Amsterdam its name and you'll be in rapidly gentrifying Oost. Once a mostly blue-collar enclave, it is rapidly becoming more and more attractive and upscale.

A bit further east you'll find the lovely Oosterpark, with a growing number of bars and restaurants on its east side (Linneausstraat) as well as the famous windmill to the north at the beginning of Zeeburgerpad. This is the place that started the Amsterdam craft brewery movement (chapter 48).

In the other direction, to the southeast of Oosterpark, is the sleepy residential Watergraafsmeer neighborhood, with beautiful 100-year-old houses. East from the railroad tracks, in the Indische Buurt / Javaplein area, things get more rough, but here too there's much buzz. Nice new restaurants, shops and condos seem to sprout out of nowhere and the yuppies have taken notice.

If you're willing to make the trek further out (get a bike, it'll be by far the easiest way to get around) check out the Flevopark, especially if it's a sunny day. This is a locals-only park without pretense. Hidden inside the park is a building that makes it own unique traditional Dutch gin, Distilleerderij 't Nieuwe Diep (chapter 51).

If you start going to the north you'll end up in the area that served as Amsterdam's main working harbor from the 1700s to the 1950s, the Eastern Docklands (*Oostelijk Havengebied*). And guess what? It's been redeveloped! Surprise.

From the Eastern Docklands it's a quick trip back to Centraal Station in the west, where you can hop a tram or train to pretty much anywhere in Amsterdam, Holland (or Europe!) or catch a free river ferry.

Across the IJ River, there are many interesting things happening in the once-staid Noord. Directly across from Centraal Station is the excellent film museum and the A'dam tower, offering great views. The NDSM area (chapter 35) is further west, but still on the North Shore. Another former harbor, the NDSM area now hosts artists and creative companies.

That's Amsterdam. Ready to explore or what?

11

Dutch Courage Required

When crossing the street beware of bikes, Amsterdam's silent killers. And trams. Cars, too. Hell, beware of runners. Pogo-stickers. Rollerbladers. Crossing the street in Amsterdam sometimes requires the timing of a train conductor, the effortless moves of a ballerina and the courage of a drunken sailor.

(But, really, really stay vigilant about those bikes.)

Inevitably, you will approach street crossings that go something like sidewalk > bike lane > car lane > tram line > tram line > car lane > bike lane > sidewalk. That means you'll be "looking both ways" six different times in one street crossing. And you're not safe until you reach the other sidewalk! Reader and fellow traveler, if you recall only one tip from this book, make it this one: The bike lane is *NOT* the sidewalk.

780,559 inhabitants / 881,000 bikes

Amsterdam is a city of bikes with some human owners. In fact, bikes outnumber residents — Amsterdam's 780,559 inhabitants own an estimated 881,000 bikes. Bikes are by far the traveler's most dangerous adversary for two reasons: They have the right of way and run as silent as a ninja in the night. Let's unpack those two facts.

Right of way. I know this sounds antithetical to my American readers, where the Rule of Gross Tonnage prevails. But everyone — cars, trams, pedestrians, cats, dogs — yields to bicycles in Amsterdam. That is, if they know what's good for them. You ought do the same. Only once your way is clear of bikers should you commence crossing.

Silence. Well, actually, Amsterdammers don't hesitate to make use of their bike bells. That said, travelers must tune their ears to a bike bell. Realize that the pleasant ring of a bike bell signifies, you know, imminent impact. Therefore, get out of the way. Are you inadvertently standing in/beside/on the corner of the bike lane? Save yourself dear traveler.

One last note on crossing the street in Amsterdam: Be so, so careful outside Centraal Station. Especially if you're just arriving all tired and jet-lagged. Packed with trams, bikers and buses, this opening foray into Amsterdam remains one of its most dangerous traffic areas.

12

De Pijp is De Bomb

The Amsterdam island, the *just-far-enough-from-the-old-center* De Pijp ("The Pipe," it's shaped like a pipe — tobacco pipe!), offers the finest combination of pleasant accommodation, quality restaurants and bars as well as proximity to Amsterdam's main attractions. In Amsterdam, De Pijp endures as my top pick for a home base.

Discovered long ago by the Lonely Planet set and having long-since outgrown its status as Amsterdam's best hidden-in-plain-sight and up-and-coming neighborhood, De Pijp remains as pleasant an area as you'll find in central Amsterdam. De Pijp — still balancing what is partly a quiet neighborhood oasis and partly a destination in its own right — hosts Europe's largest and the city's most-diverse outdoor market, the Albert Cuypmarkt (chapter 24), a beautiful park, Sarphatipark (chapter 37), and a bevy of varied restaurants and bars too numerous to list here.

From De Pijp, most Amsterdam attractions require a short walk and/or easy tram ride. Additionally, retiring to De Pijp after a big sightseeing day rewards the weary traveler with bustling restaurants serving European and international food, bars with outdoor patios and cozy coffee shops in the pedestrian zone between Sarphatipark and Albert Cuypstraat.

Once upon a time, I scored Airbnbs here for a fraction of what a hotel room cost, €50 for a single. Nowadays, prices have more than doubled, yet the constantly shifting Airbnb supply (if booked early enough) remains as strong in De Pijp as anywhere in Amsterdam. Also, high-quality, independent budget hotels in the two- and three-star range predominate in De Pijp. These are my plan B when Airbnb fails.

But the secret is out. Book your De Pijp room early.

Missed out on De Pijp rooms or think central Amsterdam isn't right? Then, the next chapter is for you.

13

Maybe You'd Prefer Haarlem?

D
oes the thought of sleeping so close to Amsterdam's Red Light District with its attendant party-hearty atmosphere turn you off? Do Amsterdam's notorious crowds give you pause? Are Amsterdam's hotel and Airbnb rates outside your budget? In other words, even though you're visiting Amsterdam, do you really want to *stay* in Amsterdam?

Just a 15-minute, nonstop train ride to Amsterdam's Centraal Station, Haarlem is within easy striking distance. You can get in and out of Amsterdam proper with nary a hassle, like a repo man in the night. However, Haarlem is no suburban afterthought. It's a worthy destination in its own right, a thriving university town with gobsmacking churches, a lovely mix of traditional and modern Dutch architecture, excellent dining options and a quaint shopping district.

Dutch master Frans Hals called Haarlem home — visit the eponymous museum. Marvel at St. Bavo Church. Mozart once played the organ here, a fact you can't escape Haarlem without learning. Also, the amazing boutique shopping includes one of the world's cutest independent bookstores, Bookstore H. de

Vries Books. And you'll find tasty and authentic French fries at the steeped-in-tradition Frietkamer. Lastly, wash down those salty taters with a craft beer at the glorious Jopenkerk, a brewery holed up in a 15th-century church.

So, maybe you'd prefer Haarlem?

14

Safety Meeting

I nevitably, after raving about one of the greatest cities in the world, I'm asked, "Is Amsterdam safe?"

It's a knee-jerk reaction that always catches me off-guard. Maybe it's the quasi-legal pot, tolerated hallucinogens, legal prostitution? Or could it be the rising sea level constantly imperiling the city's future? I don't know! (I bet it's not the climate change one, though.)

But I do know you may be a little apprehensive about seeing Amsterdam because of its liberal reputation (whores, weed and whatnot). However, Amsterdam is actually considered the sixth-safest city in the world, according to the 2017 Safe Cities Index, making it the highest-ranked European city. Even though Amsterdam is safe, it never hurts to reiterate a few key precautions.

Pickpockets & tourist scams

Be aware of possible pickpockets and scam artists. Keep your personal belongings in front of you, hidden or secured. Avoid carrying backpacks or large shoulder bags that someone could easily open without you knowing. Don't store all your cash in one pocket. Instead, split it into a couple (front-facing, preferably) pockets and your day bag/money belt/document holder.

Be cautious in the Red Light District after nightfall, when pickpockets like to make their profit. Another place to watch out for pickpockets is, of course, on the tram or train since you may be in close proximity to a lot of people.

One Amsterdam scam aimed at tourists is fake taxis at the airport. Do not grab a random taxi when you get off the plane because it could be someone who wants to take you out-of-town to rob you or, worse, *OVERCHARGE* you. Use Amsterdam's fabulous public transportation or hire a taxi from the official stand in front of Schiphol Plaza.

Canal smarts

Street smarts are important no matter what new city you decide to explore. Specifically, to stay safe in Amsterdam you should be wary of canals, especially if you've been imbibing. Even though it may be tempting to cool off in a canal, it is actually illegal...and disgusting. Don't get too close or lean over bridge railings if you've had a few too many.

So, is Amsterdam safe? The answer is yes, a million times yes. As long as you use common sense and are aware of your surroundings you should be safe in Amsterdam. Having knowledge of areas in the city will help to boost your feeling of safety as well as traveling with another person or a group of people.

15

Amsterdam's Hotspots

Y ou might be unsurprised to learn Amsterdam is well connected — like its northern European neighbors — and finding free wifi in Amsterdam will be one of the easiest errands of your trip. While visiting the city you will be able to stay connected to friends, family and, most importantly, your Instagram followers.

Where to find free wifi in Amsterdam

Most major hubs of transportation offer free wifi for public use. Consequently, if you're flying into Schiphol Airport, they have wifi. Passengers arriving at Centraal Station, Amsterdam's main train station, will also find free wifi.

Wifi services exist in many of the well-known tourist attractions, museums and coffee houses. Places like the Van Gogh Museum, Rijksmuseum and Anne Frank House are all equipped with fast and free wifi. Of course, the usual suspects like McDonald's, Starbucks and Bagels & Beans supply free wifi as well. Most public libraries have wifi and the American Book

36

Center, located at Spui 12, provides connectivity as well as a nice spot to read, write and shop.

Tools for finding free wifi in Amsterdam

Use one of the following websites and apps to score free wifi in Amsterdam. Remember, hotspots change — some go paid, others go dark. Similarly, power outlets are available at some but not all hotspots. Finally, you will sometimes have to ask at the counter or reception for an access code.

- Wifi Amsterdam will give you a list of over 90 locations offering free wifi in the Amsterdam. The interactive map allows you to find the closest wifi location.
- FON is a wifi community in which members share their wireless access with other members. In exchange, members are able to use any wifi access point in this community. You must buy a special router if you want to use FON. Even if you decide not to share your internet access, you can still use FON by purchasing a card from them.
- The Your Little Black Book app reveals over 800 hotspots in the city.

16

Going Cashless & Contactless

Amsterdam is tech savvy. Perhaps you've picked up on this trend.

Now, it's time to really drive home the point: Amsterdam, like its northern European and Scandinavian brethren, is fast ditching cash in favor of digital payments. Placed over a scanner instead of swiping or inserting, RFID-enabled "contactless" credit cards and "smart pay/virtual wallet"-enabled smartphones rule the retail landscape. Yes, dear reader, from restaurants and museums to public trams and buses, Amsterdam prefers the cashless, contactless transaction.

In fact, you can no longer purchase tram or bus passes on-board using cash — cards only. When it comes to tickets, many museums nowadays strongly prefer or outright require online booking — including the highly recommended Anne Frank House. All over Amsterdam, retail establishments aren't only set up for contactless transactions, they prefer it. Restaurants? Bars? Same. Same.

What can a traveler do? Well, obviously, bring a credit card or two. While you may not have access to contactless cards, do remember to attach travel plans and set the pin numbers before departing. If you already utilize a contactless payment system on your phone like Apple Pay, then you're in luck. Contactless payments are accepted just about everywhere. If not, then your Amsterdam trip provides a good excuse to start.

All that said, the Red Light District, its many derivatives and temptations — pot shops, strip clubs, smart shops and sex workers — almost universally require good old cash-money euros.

But outside the vice quarters, this city is quickly going cash-less.

17

Predicting the Unpredictable

msterdam enjoys a mild, Mediterranean climate...just kidding! Amsterdam weather, due to its location on the North Sea, somewhat *in* the North Sea, means temperatures and forecasts swing dramatically. Cold, wet, fierce storms blow in from the North Sea seemingly out of nowhere.

In short, Amsterdam's weather is unpredictable. It's best to keep an eye on forecasts immediately before and during your trip. That said, here's a look at Amsterdam's seasonal weather with corresponding clothing recommendations. Just don't go writing any of this in stone...

Summer

In general, summer in Amsterdam is warm, but not uncomfortably hot or humid. However, there are occasionally days when you could be sweating. Rain is common in Amsterdam in the summer, which can make planning outdoor activities a bit dicey.

- **Average temperature:** 69 degrees Fahrenheit / 21 degrees Celsius
- **Average precipitation:** ~7 inches / 186 millimeters from June–August
- **Average daylight hours:** 16.25 hours

What to wear: Amsterdam clothing is typically pretty casual, especially for a big European city. Summer is a good time to wear skirts, shorts, light jeans, short-sleeved shirts and dresses. Toward the beginning of summer, it's also a good idea to bring along a light jacket or sweatshirt. Because rain falls erratically, an umbrella is also an essential part of your summer kit.

Fall

Fall in Amsterdam starts out on a pleasant note with the warmth and sunshine of summer sticking around. However, as the season progresses, the weather grows colder, wetter, windier and grayer. In mid-to-late fall, Amsterdam begins to see its first night frosts.

- **Average temperature:** 58 degrees Fahrenheit / 14 degrees Celsius
- **Average precipitation:** ~8.5 inches / 219 millimeters from September–November
- **Average daylight hours:** 10.5 hours

What to wear: In an already wet city, fall is easily the wettest time in Amsterdam. Arrive prepared with rain gear, waterproof shoes and extra socks. A sturdy umbrella is also a good idea, as harsh winds can mangle cheap ones. Temperatures can fluctuate but tend to be on the colder side. Fall is a good time to dress in layers, such as jeans and long underwear with a light sweater and a jacket.

Winter

Winter weather in Amsterdam tends to be quite cold and windy. However, this can vary depending on which way the winds are blowing. Winds from the west can bring warmer temperatures, but winds from the east can make it terribly cold. There is quite a bit of precipitation, including snow, rain and sleet. While precipitation falls frequently, the amounts per occurrence tend to stay low.

- **Average temperature:** 43 degrees Fahrenheit / 6 degrees Celsius
- **Average precipitation:** ~7 inches / 177mm from December–February
- **Average daylight hours:** 8 hours

What to wear: Amsterdam becomes bitingly cold in winter. The city remains quite wet in winter, so a waterproof jacket and shoes are essential. To keep yourself protected against the cold, pack layers of warm sweaters, long underwear, hat, scarf and gloves, as well as thick long pants.

Spring

Spring starts out rather cold, with temperatures similar to those of the winter months. Amsterdam sometimes experiences light snow in the early days of spring. However, April and May are typically some of the most pleasant months in Amsterdam, with warming temperatures and brilliantly long days.

- **Average temperature:** 56 degrees Fahrenheit / 13 degrees Celsius
- **Average precipitation:** ~6.25 / 159 millimeters from March–May
- **Average daylight hours:** 13.5 hours

What to wear: Spring is an erratic time for Amsterdam weather. Temperatures vary significantly, so dress in light layers. A good mix is jeans with a light shirt and a sweater and/or jacket. Spring is also very wet, so an umbrella or other rain gear is a good idea.

Umbrella. Rain gear. Are you seeing the pattern?

18

Everyday Carry: Your Passport

The Kingdom of the Netherlands prides itself on running a liberal democracy. Yet, here are two words that may send shivers down your freedom-loving spine: compulsory identification.

But don't freak out. Or, rather, read on before you do.

The law

Netherlands law requires residents and foreign nationals to show valid ID if asked by:
- police officers,
- ticket inspectors on public transport,
- special enforcement officers (BOAs) like labour inspectors and forest wardens.

These officials must provide reasoning, justification before asking for ID. In other words, they won't randomly stop you for an ID shakedown. Amsterdam isn't Moscow. Law requires they be investigating a crime, managing transportation or

— and this is the one travelers should know — maintaining public order. Yes, that could be you, heavily intoxicated tourist. Disturbing the peace, are we?

Failure to show valid ID results in a fine of €60 for people 16 and over or €30 for teens 14-15. That's a lot of dough in a city as pricey as Amsterdam, where you want to stretch every euro.

Look, you and I both know you're not the type to get all publicly intoxicated and cause a scene. However, you are a law-abiding traveler. Right? So, you do need to follow the rules and laws governing the countries in which you travel. Therefore, even if you don't plan on causing a ruckus (and definitely if you do!), carry your passport on your person in Amsterdam.

II

Go >> See >> Do

Avoiding lines, and other tips and tricks for maximizing your Amsterdam sightseeing.

19

One Museum Pass to Rule Them All

Traveling Amsterdam without one of the three following Amsterdam museum passes is a fool's errand. I wouldn't wish it upon even my worst enemies. Dramatic enough? Well, now that you're surely on board with the idea of buying a museum pass, let's review the options. We start with the best of the lot, the Iamsterdam City Card. Without a doubt, every tourist should consider buying this pass.

Iamsterdam City Card

- **Price:** €59 for 24 hours, €74 for 48 hours, €84 for 72 hours, €98 for 96 hours
- **Main Benefits:** Access to over 60 attractions, unlimited public transportation, free one-hour canal tour, discounts at local restaurants & shops
- **Best For:** Trips less than a week, travelers utilizing public transport, fast & furious sightseers
- Website

This easy-to-use card allows you to walk freely into 60 of the Amsterdam's top attractions. Even more, it'll help get you get there. That's right, an Iamsterdam City Card allows users free access on Amsterdam's GVB public transportation system, which includes buses, trams and the metro. Plus, the Iamsterdam City Card entitles you to a free one-hour canal tour from any of the cruise lines that work with Iamsterdam.

The two most-prominent museums featured on this card are the Van Gogh Museum and the Rijksmuseum. A few other cool places you can check out include the Tropenmuseum, the Rembrandt House Museum and (for those who are feeling lucky) the Holland Casino Amsterdam.

One slight drawback to this card is that it doesn't offer access to the popular Anne Frank House. On the flip side, this card gives you numerous discounts at many fabulous attractions and tours around the city including classical concerts at the Het Concertgebouw, tickets to hop-on-hop-off buses and the Heineken Experience. The Iamsterdam card offers undoubtedly the greatest value of all Amsterdam museum passes. It's best for travelers seeking the "full package."

Amsterdam Museum Card

- **Price:** €64.90 for ages 19+, €32.45 for ages 18 and under
- **Main Benefits:** Access to over 400 museums in the Netherlands, five museum visits within 31 days, includes Anne Frank House, skip-the-line access in certain museums
- **Best For:** Trips a week or more, Anne Frank House, day trips outside Amsterdam, slower travelers
- Website

While visitors to Amsterdam aren't barred from purchasing "*Museumkaarts*," these aren't one of the more tourist-friendly Amsterdam museum passes. For starters, you can't order this card online if you live outside of the Netherlands. Secondly, this card's website is all in Dutch...and let's face it, sometimes things get lost in Google Translation. Third, and perhaps most important, foreign tourists can only use this card at five of 400 participating museums within a 31-day period. This is a huge bummer, especially considering the Dutch get to use their museum cards for unlimited access to museums *within a year*. Bear in mind, however, that this card has always been targeted to the local market.

Despite these drawbacks, consider buying an Amsterdam Museum Card if you plan on visiting exactly five major museums. And/or you're keen to explore outside of Amsterdam. As a tourist, you will have to purchase a "*Museumkaart*" at one of Amsterdam's top 22 museums. Locations include the Amsterdam Museum, the Van Gogh Museum, the Rijksmuseum and more. Also, keep in mind that these cards entitle you to skip-the-line privileges at certain museums.

Unlike the Iamsterdam card, you can get into the Anne Frank House with one of these Amsterdam museum passes. Since the Anne Frank House is one of the most popular Amsterdam museums, however, reserve a visit time online for an extra €0.50. A few other fascinating museums that accept this museum pass include the following: the Zeeuws Museum, the Airborn Museum 'Hartenstein,' the Portuguese Synagogue, the Oude Kerk and the EYE Film Museum.

Amsterdam Holland Pass

- **Price:** €40 for small, €55 for medium, €71.25 for large
- **Main Benefits:** Free or discounted access to over 80 attractions, discount card, valid for one month after first use, can be used in over ten Dutch cities, easy pre-order portal online, free guidebook included
- **Best For:** Trips a week or more, savvy museum-goers, day trips outside Amsterdam
- Website

Amsterdam Holland Passes are split into three categories: small, medium and large. How many attractions you get to enter for free remains the main differentiator. Small card users receive free entrance to one gold and one silver attraction. Medium users get four free entrances (two gold and two silver). Large card owners get six free entrances (three gold and three silver). All Holland Passes are valid for one month after you swipe it for the first time.

By now you're probably asking, "*So what's the deal with gold and silver attractions? Is this the Olympics?*" Basically, the attractions listed in the golden category average more visitors. In total, the pass guarantees access to 80 attractions in about ten of Holland's top cities like Amsterdam, Utrecht and Rotterdam.

While there are the big-name museums such as the Rijksmuseum (gold) and Van Gogh Museum (silver) available on every Amsterdam Holland Pass, you could also use your gold/silver credits for complimentary experiences like a one-hour canal tour, a tour of the Johan Cruijff Arena or a three-hour bike rental. Once you're done using up your gold/silver points, it's time to break out your discount card. Lastly, all Holland Passes come with a discount card for certain restaurants, entertainment venues and museums. Note: the Anne Frank House is not included on these passes.

20

Bought Anne Frank House Tickets Yet?

T his house hid the Frank family from the Nazis for two years during World War II. The family would silently sit in their home during the day, until they were mysteriously betrayed and shipped off to Nazi concentration camps. Fifteen-year-old Anne Frank recorded the story of their survival during that two-year period in her diary. Otto Frank later published Anne's diary in 1947. He was the only Frank to survive the war.

No first trip to Amsterdam is complete without visiting the Anne Frank House. Now almost 60 years after opening as a museum, the Anne Frank House remains one of Europe's most-important and emotionally charged sites. However, buying Anne Frank House tickets requires a little advanced planning.

Before arriving, you should reserve ahead for the Anne Frank House. Anne Frank House tickets are only sold online and are assigned to specific dates and times. Reservations are non-transferable, so make sure you know exactly when you want to visit and commit.

How to buy Anne Frank House tickets online

Reservations for the Anne Frank House must be made online, preferably prior to your visit. This is the only way to purchase your tickets. Click here to buy your Anne Frank House tickets.

The museum caps daily visits and releases 80% of a given day's tickets online two months in advance. They dispense the other 20% on the day of. Therefore, you have a much better chance of securing a desired date and time by booking online in advance.

If tickets are unavailable for a specific day, the website will show the message, "Unfortunately, no more tickets available" on the selected date. You can risk buying your Anne Frank House tickets on the day of your visit online. Just find some wifi and purchase from the website. However, keep in mind that tickets do sell out quickly.

How to buy Anne Frank House tickets on-site

As of publication time in late 2018, you can't. Unfortunately, Anne Frank House tickets are only available for purchase online.

Pricing for Anne Frank House reservations

Accurate as of October, 2018
- **Adults 18 & over:** €10
- **Kids 10-17:** €5
- **Kids 0-9:** free
- **Booking fee per ticket:** €0.50

Additional entrance options:

- **Museumkaart:** free**
- **EYCA:** €5**

**0.50 booking charge still applies.

A quick recap

- Anne Frank House tickets must be purchased online from the official website up to two months in advance.
- The Anne Frank House website charges a €.50 booking fee per ticket.
- Anne Frank house tickets are non-transferable and non-refundable.
- Tickets are assigned a specific entry date and time.
- The museum caps daily visits and releases 80% of a given day's tickets online two months in advance. The remaining 20% go up for sale the day of.

That's it. Now grab a box or two of tissues and go experience the Anne Frank House for yourself.

21

Ditto: Van Gogh Tickets?

L ocated in the heart of Amsterdam's museum district on the airy Museumplein, the Van Gogh Museum boasts the largest collection of works attributed to the illustrious Dutch painter, Vincent Van Gogh. With 200 paintings, 400 drawings and 700 letters on display, the Van Gogh remains the most-visited museum in Amsterdam and the Netherlands. As a result of its popularity, you should know how to buy Van Gogh Museum tickets in advance.

How to buy tickets in Amsterdam

As the museum is busy almost any time of day, visiting the Van Gogh Museum requires you reserve ahead. That said, you can buy tickets once in Amsterdam online or at a tourist office. Holders of Museumkaart passes or the Iamsterdam card can purchase tickets for free online or at any of Amsterdam's tourist offices. For other visitors, you can buy skip the line tickets for the Van Gogh museum by making time-dependent reservations at any of Amsterdam's Iamsterdam tourist offices. The most-convenient tourist office might be the one located right outside Amsterdam's Centraal train station. However, be prepared to wait since the tourist offices typically experience long lines.

Buying online

Start by going to the Van Gogh Museum website. Select the number of visitors and the day and time of your visit. If your plans change, you may cancel or change up to two weeks beforehand, free of charge. After that, you must pay full price. Guided group tours and multimedia guides are optional.

Pricing

Adult tickets cost €18. Children under 18 can obtain tickets for free. Companion tickets are also complimentary. For example, if a patron is unable to navigate the museum on his or her own, he or she may bring a companion.

A quick recap

- Van Gogh Museum reservations are free with the Museumkaart pass or Iamsterdam card.
- Purchase tickets online up to four months in advance.
- Adult tickets cost €18, while children 18 and under visit free.
- Both printed and digital tickets are accepted.
- Your ticket is only valid on the selected date and time.
- You can enter the museum up to 30 minutes after your reserved starting time.
- Van Gogh Museum opens daily from 9AM to 5PM and until 10PM on Fridays. Expect later closing times in spring,

summer and over the winter holidays.

22

An Homage to Rembrandt

C onnect with Amsterdam's artistic past and immerse yourself in visceral history at the Rembrandt House Museum. This historic building was the home and workshop of famous artist and former Amsterdam resident, Rembrandt Harmenszoon van Rijn, during the 20 years between 1639 and 1658.

History

The construction of the original Rembrandt House in Amsterdam was completed in 1607 in an area of the city once known as Sint Anthonisbreestraat. Rembrandt purchased the home in 1639 and after going through years of financial trouble he was forced into bankruptcy. The house was auctioned in 1658; it changed owners and significantly deteriorated over the next couple of centuries. In 1906 the City of Amsterdam bought the building and spent the next five years restoring it to its former glory and Queen Wilhelmina opened the museum in 1911. The museum's collection expanded over the last century and they built an annex to house more exhibits in the 1990s.

Location

The Rembrandt House Museum is located in the heart of old Amsterdam next to Waterlooplein Square, which is about a 15 minute walk from the Dam Square. If you are riding the tram, you can exit at the Waterlooplein stop from lines 9 and 14.

Collection

The core of the collection at the Rembrandt House includes Rembrandt's graphical work, as well as the work of other artists who used the studio before and during the time Rembrandt worked and lived there. The museum holds 260 of Rembrandt's etchings and a selection of drawings and copper plates.

Hours

The museum is open daily from 10AM to 6PM except for December 25 (Christmas Day) and April 27 (King's Day). On New Year's Eve and Christmas Eve, the museum typically closes early at 5PM. On New Year's Day the museum opens at 11AM.

Tickets

You can purchase tickets online at the Rembrandt House Museum website. Adults cost €13, ages 6–17 cost €4 and children up to five and students go free. If you have an Iamsterdam city card, Museumkaart or ICON card, then your admission is also free.

23

Can Kiddos Go Free?

While Amsterdam's museums lack the free accommodation afforded children in other European cities, like London, Paris and Berlin, free entrances for kids and teens do indeed exist. The list below details major recommended Amsterdam museums along with which ages gain free admission. (I've boldfaced the attractions I find most worthwhile.)

Luckily, four of what I consider the city's top six attractions offer free entrance to under 18s — Rijksmuseum, Stedelijk, Royal Palace and Van Gogh. The two notable holdouts — the Anne Frank House and Dutch Resistance Museum — do at least let little kids in gratis. However, I'm not recommending the Anne Frank House for kids under 10, though that wholly depends on maturity level. On the other hand, the Dutch Resistance Museum runs a wonderfully interactive "junior" museum. It's not only worth the price of admission but it's also the leading reason why the museum charges for kids.

Major Amsterdam museums and what ages get in free:

1. **Rijksmuseum: 0-18**
2. **Stedelijk: 0-18**
3. Amsterdam Museum: 0-17
4. **Royal Palace: 0-17**
5. **Van Gogh Museum: 0-17**
6. Oude Kerk: 0-12
7. Hermitage Amsterdam: 0-11
8. Nieuwe Kerk: 0-11
9. **Anne Frank House: 0-9**
10. **Dutch Resistance Museum: 0-6**
11. Canal House Museum: 0-5
12. MOCO Museum: 0-5
13. **Rembrandt House: 0-5**
14. Biblical Museum: 0-4
15. Houseboat Museum: 0-4
16. **Ons' Lieve Heer op Solder: 0-4**

24

Resistance is Futile

Amsterdam is a hive of world-class museums, and the Verzetsmuseum, the Dutch Resistance Museum, shines bright among the gems. In fact, critics christened it the Netherland's best historical museum.

History

Between 1940 and 1945, Nazi Germany occupied the Netherlands. The occupation sparked a predominately nonviolent movement known as the Dutch resistance. Via interactive installations enhanced with temporary and permanent exhibits, patrons get a comprehensive education on how the Dutch people responded to the foreign invasion. The museum was born of a 1980 exhibit called 1933-19now. By 1984, the venture had morphed into a standalone museum.

Collection

The Dutch resistance museum maintains a permanent collection of documents, artifacts and artworks that serve to memorialize the movement. Guided docent tours and (FREE!) highly recommend, self-guided audio tours are also available.

Risk of Explosion!

The Dutch Resistance was a predominately nonviolent endeavor. However, in 1943, a group of disguised artists and students attacked the Amsterdam Registry Office in a physical show of defiance. This exhibit commemorates the event via an interactive experience.

The Junior Museum

Credited as the first children's museum about World War II, the Verzetsmuseum's "Junior Museum" is an interactive journey through the lives of Henk, Eva, Jan and Nelly, four kids who lived in the Netherlands during the occupation. However, please note that parents are encouraged to leave children younger than nine at home.

Logistics

Do you like immersive historical experiences? If so, then do the Anne Frank walk. It starts at her house and ends at the museum. Along the way, you'll see and learn about important landmarks associated with Ms. Frank and the Dutch resistance.

Do you prefer taking public transportation? From Centraal

Station take tram #14. The Artis Zoo stop is closest. The 51, 53 and 54 metro lines will take you to the Waterlooplein/Uitgang Hortus stop, just a short walk to the venue.

The museum is open daily from 10/11AM to 5PM. You can buy tickets online or at the door. Save for a few situational anomalies, tickets sell for:

- **Adults:** €11
- **Kids 7-16 years:** €6
- **Students:** €6
- **Family entry:** €26
- **iAmsterdam and Museumkaart:** Free entry

25

Swinging Amsterdam

No, ahem, not that kind of swinging. You are forgiven, of course, for assuming such notions. After all, this is Amsterdam. I'm sorry to disappoint. Instead, I'm talking about actual, literal swinging on a swing. Wait! Don't go! It's really cool!

Behind Centraal Station, you'll find three free ferries plying the IJ River. Take ferry #901, the one headed toward Buiksloterweg, which crosses the river straight to the stunning Eye Cinema / Film Museum and A'dam Tower in about 5 minutes. This tower includes bars, clubs and restaurants for ever-growing hipster Amsterdam. But skip that and go straight to the roof. Here, you'll find a swing aptly called "Over The Edge." For €5 you get strapped in and face your vertigo when swinging out over Amsterdam from 22 floors up. Touted as Europe's highest swing, it's one high from Amsterdam you may actually remember.

26

Boat Tours to the Canals & Beyond

Canal tours provide travelers with the most stunning views of Amsterdam. Traveling by boat on Amsterdam's canals adds a magical touch to your exploration. It's also an efficient and memorable way to orient yourself to the city and its many canal-side neighborhoods and attractions.

Really, the hardest part is choosing a company because you will be inundated quite literally the moment you step out from Centraal Station. Most companies run the standard couple of loops or offer a hop-on, hop-off route through Amsterdam's canals. You can't go wrong with these tours. However, a few unconventional standout options include:

Evening canal cruise

During this 90-minute tour you get to view the beautiful city bejeweled with street lights underneath a starry sky. The route passes the city's major historic spots along the Golden Bend, Skinny Bridge and much more.

Small boat canal cruise

Throughout this unique, hour-long boat adventure, you will see beautiful, 17th-century merchant houses, old churches, bridges and houseboats. This canal cruise runs from March to early November.

Private day trip from Amsterdam to Giethoorn

For a more intimate cruising experience, spend up to eight hours touring the town of Giethoorn. Since this tour is private, your schedule is very flexible and can be customized to your needs.

27

Choose Your Own Canal Adventure

How could you turn down the chance to spend a clear, sunny day cruising the relaxing Amsterdam canals with your closest friends, family members and travel buddies? You can't! Renting an electric boat doesn't require a captain's license and is by far the most fun way for groups and independent-minded travelers to tour the canals. Here are a few established shops that rent safe and easy-to-skipper electric boats.

Mokumboot

With Mokum, you can rent boats that fit eight people for up to four hours. They rent from six different locations around Amsterdam. Powered by quiet electric motors, Mokum's boats also have standard steering wheels, which make them easy to drive even for beginners.

Rates:
- 2 hours: €90
- 3 hours: €110

- 4 hours: €140

Boaty

Located on De Pijp in south-central Amsterdam, Boaty rents out six-person electric boats that are roofed with solar panels. So, you never have to worry about sun beaming on your head or losing power (at least on sunny days).

Rates are somewhat complicated, ranging from €79 for three hours to €219 for a full day.

Canal Motorboats Amsterdam

Claiming to be Amsterdam's oldest boat-rental company, Canal Motorboats Amsterdam is certainly the most centrally located, just steps from Centraal Station. Their boats accommodate up to seven people. Canal Motorboats is open all year, weather permitting. Prices vary depending on time.

Rates:
- First hour: €50
- Second hour: €40
- Third hour: €30
- Fourth hour: €20
- Each subsequent hour costs €20

A couple caveats

In order to drive a rental boat, you must be at least 18 years old with valid identification, pay the full rental cost at time of booking and be prepared to provide a deposit of at least €100 in cash or pre-authorized on a credit card.

28

Shop the Jordaan's "9 Straatjes"

Not keen on boats? Or want another way to experience Amsterdam's scenic canals? How about going shopping? You see, shopping along Amsterdam's canals is an activity even a landlubber will enjoy. Amsterdam's most popular canal shopping area sits around nine little streets in the picturesque Jordaan District, called aptly enough Amsterdam's 9 Streets (*"Straatjes"*). The 9 Streets cross two iconic Amsterdam canals: Herengracht and Keizersgracht. West of these two canals lies Prinsengracht canal while Singel canal sits to the East.

On Amsterdam's 9 Streets, you'll find locals and tourists alike perusing, elbow-to-elbow, clothing boutiques, eating at nice restaurants and canal-side cafes, visiting bookshops and even getting their hair done. For travelers on a tight budget, good news, no purchase required. Anyone can come enjoy the atmospheric 9 Streets district, strolling and window shopping till your heart is content and your wallet no lighter. In fact, while I always come here, I don't think I've ever bought anything other than food and drink.

Here's a rundown of each street and what you'll find:

1. **Reestraat:** Reestraat is known for clothing and home-decorating shops. However, this street would not be complete without two fine restaurants, the Amsterdam Watch Company and an art gallery, Galeria Lughien.

2. **Hartenstraat:** Fashion and home-decorating stores flood the street, along with a Karl Lagerfeld boutique as the stamp, complete with a couple of small restaurants.

3. **Gasthuismolensteeg:** This street hosts National Museum of Spectacles, several clothing shops, long-standing casual sandwich shops and designer shoe boutiques.

4. **Berenstraat:** The street known for eating and shopping. The major points on the street are the popular cafe, t'Zwaantje, the lingerie boutique by Marlies Dekkers, and a unique, all-black bookshop Mendo. Also, several fashion outlets.

5. **Wolvenstraat:** Wolvenstraat consists of many upscale fashion boutiques, vintage clothing stores, beauty parlors and cafes. This is one of the most popular streets in the city. You will experience crowds.

6. **Oude Spielgelstraat:** Handbag stores, like Bags by Rika, Margaret M and another shop by French couturier L'Etoile de Saint Honore take over this street, along with an antique shop.

7. **Runstraat:** This street is normally busy at most times of day due to two beauty salons, restaurants and a popular, old-fashioned Grand Cafe that doesn't close until 4AM.

8. **Huidenstraat:** Another buzzing street packed with crowds, Huidenstraat offers a range of options from restaurants to fashion, jewelry and accessory shops.

9. **Wijde Heisteg:** This is the shortest of the nine streets, with

a mixture of clothing shops, lunchrooms, a hairdresser and jewelry store.

29

"Tourist" Tram Lines

Many Amsterdam experts tout tram #2 as the city's de facto "tourist" line because it links so many beautiful neighborhoods and top sights. Even GVB, Amsterdam's public-transportation authority, describes it as such here. Rightly so. It's a wonderful ride.

However, I also enthusiastically recommend tram line #3. Other than the old city center, it connects many of the same areas as #2 but adds several up-and-coming, modern and hipster neighborhoods. Which means good food. And good beard-watching.

Tram #3 runs east-west while #2 runs north-south; the lines intersect at the Van Baerlestraat stop. Between the two tram lines, you're never more than a couple of lovely blocks from a main attraction, making them just about the only lines a traveler needs to know. I like to buy a 24-hour pass and really cover some ground, punctuating my rides with long walks.

Tram #2

Departing from Centraal Station, tram #2 bisects the center of old Amsterdam running south, past the inner canal ring en route to Vondelpark and Museumplein, home to the Rijks, Stedelijk and Van Gogh museums. The line continues into southwestern Amsterdam, but the furthest most travelers ride is the Amstelveenseweg stop.

To explore the famous Jordaan and inner canals, get out at either Keizersgracht or Prinsengracht stops and head northwest. Exit at Rijksmuseum for the, you guessed it, Rijksmuseum. Get out at Van Baerlestraat for the Stedelijk and Van Gogh.

For a fun, self-guided morning, ride the tram from Centraal Station out to Amstelveenseweg. Then walk back toward old town through Vondelpark, stopping at Museumplein (book museum tickets in advance), the Jordaan and, finally, the old center. For this plan of attack, a single-ride ticket is sufficient. If you grow tired of walking, simply hop back on the #2 heading north toward Centraal Station. Do it in reverse if you're staying outside the center.

Tram #3

While tram line #3 isn't a classic Amsterdam tourist tram line, it does link three redeveloped hipster/yuppie areas with the city's best markets, Noordermarkt and Albert Cuypmarkt. Plus, like #2, it'll also deposit you at Vondelpark and the museums.

Tram #3 skirts the city center, staying mostly outside the Singel canal. Originating near Westerpark in the west #3, runs all the way over to the architecturally splendid, glass-and-steel Eastern Docklands neighborhood. Both offer a fascinating look at how Amsterdam redeveloped its outer boroughs into trendy live-work-play neighborhoods. Or, as my son discovered, "It's where the real people live."

For the recommended Noordermarkt and Jordaan district, exit at Nw. Willemsstraat. Depart at Van Baerlestraat for Vondelpark, Stedelijk and Van Gogh museums. To explore De Pijp, Sarphatipark and Europe's largest outdoor market, Albert Cuypmarkt, hop off at the 2e v.d.Helststraat stop. For the Eastern Docklands, ride the tram to Insulindeweg. Or take it all the way to Flevopark for a locals-only scene and secret distillery (chapter 52).

30

Stealing Stopera

Amsterdam's modern opera house, the Stopera, also hosts city hall, the country's national ballet and visiting orchestras from around the world. While the building itself won't win any architectural awards, the interior acoustics are fabulous. In fact, the sound travels so well throughout the building during live performances, there's no need to even buy a ticket.

Instead, grab a coffee, wine or beer at the cozy bar nearest the main entrance. The sound travels through the ceilings, supplemented by a few speakers. Sit back and listen to the entire show while catching some free wifi or carrying on a conversation and enjoying drinks. This bar remains open until about a half hour after the performance ends.

31

Amsterdam's Clandestine Catholic Church

H idden away in Amsterdam, Our Lord in the Attic Museum thrusts visitors back in time hundreds of years.

In what outwardly appears to be an ordinary canal house, lies a secret that goes back over three centuries. Step inside. After exploring the various stately rooms with period-furnishings of this house-turned museum, climb the narrow and steep staircase to the upper floors to discover an amazing spectacle: a miniature Catholic church. But, shh, don't tell.

Our Lord in the Attic

Known as "Our Lord in the Attic" or "*Ons' Lieve Heer op Solder*," it features a beautiful gilded-gold altar, renaissance-era paintings and balcony pews that soar to two levels. Above all, it's an incredible piece of architecture built inside the space of a common attic.

The church captures the essence of the Dutch Golden Age: a

time when religious, intellectual, philosophical and scientific tolerance won the day.

History

The persecution of Catholicism and other minority faiths in 17th-century Holland forced its parishioners to worship away from public view. In the wake of Reformation throughout Europe, they were tolerated only as much as they were discreet. These hidden churches and temples provided a place among the faithful to practice their holy traditions, as officials mostly turned a blind-eye. This fully-realized Catholic church, hidden away in such a nondescript Amsterdam location, speaks to the power of faith and ingenuity.

In the late 18th century, Our Lord in the Attic converted into a museum, making it now the second oldest in the city. Over 80,000 people visit annually and there are regular religious services as well.

Among the faithful or the curious, *Ons' Lieve Heer op Solder* is a glorious sight to behold.

Travel information

- Located at Oudezijds Voorburgwal 40, 1012 GE Amsterdam.
- Hours are 10AM to 5PM Monday through Saturday; 1PM to 5PM on Sundays and holidays. The museum closes on April 27 (King's Day).
- Ticket prices are €11 adult, €5.50 children (5-17). You can purchase tickets in advance at their website or at the museum. For more information, call +31 20 624 6604.
- The museum offers guided tours in English, Dutch, German

and French.
- Catholic Mass is held every Sunday.

32

Red Light District Etiquette

While I mentioned that you should watch out for pickpockets in the central Red Light District (RLD) at night back in chapter 14, the scene is totally different during the day. During the day you will find large tourist crowds and great places to shop and dine. Let's be real, though: The pickpockets still operate during the daytime. Yet, it's a wondrously venerable and immensely interesting place to explore. Even if the whole idea of the RLD makes you squeamish, I extol a morning or afternoon walk through this tangled quarter.

Of course, there are still unwritten rules you should abide by in the RLD:

- As rollicking as it seems, people actually live in Amsterdam's Red Light District. Don't yell in the streets or drink and smoke outside late into the night.
- Do not take pictures of the prostitutes. This is a big no-no.
- If you ogle the prostitutes long enough, then you'll be not-so-kindly asked to leave by a surly man with bulging muscles.

- Know what the lights mean: If the lights in a prostitute's windows are red, she's female. Blue or mostly blue? That means she's usually a transvestite or a transitioning transexual.
- Refrain from riding your bicycle on the sidewalks. This goes for all of Amsterdam, but is especially important in the crowded and narrow Red Light District.
- Don't purchase drugs off the street. There are plenty of drugs available in the shops.
- Smoke weed in the myriad coffee shops, not out in the streets.

33

The Parakeets Who Call Amsterdam Home

T raditionally associated with the world's more tropical climes, Amsterdam's parakeets now flourish in the canal city's rooftops and parks. No, you're not tripping (yet...), I said parakeets. You know, "parrots." The kind that sit on pirates' shoulders.

With their beauty, intelligence and ability to mimic human speech, humans adore parakeets, anointing them one of the most popular avian pets in the world. Although many owners love and cherish their parakeets, others have found their way to freedom. Or endeavored their own damn way to freedom. This is certainly the case in Amsterdam, where a huge feral population now runs rampant.

History

In Amsterdam, parakeets began their Great Escape in the 1970s. There are several theories about their establishment, including that:

- someone intentionally released a breeding pair in massive Vondelpark,
- a truck carrying parakeets turned over, releasing the birds from their cages,
- and that an American company relocating to the area accidentally released dozens of birds. [Ed. *Why?!?*]

Instead of suffering from the urban environment, however, parakeets grew accustomed to easy city living. In fact, they now number some 4,000. Parakeets of Amsterdam have proven adaptable and audacious. They survive by eating fruits from Amsterdam's gardens and seed from bird feeders.

Where to find these parakeets

Looking to spot these incongruous avians for yourself? Today, Amsterdam's parakeets live, eat and breed all over the city. (Utrecht, The Hague and Rotterdam also boast their own feral-keet populations.) Sightings abound in the city's parks, including Vondelpark and Oosterpark. Like most birds, Amsterdam's parakeets tend to roost off the ground. That means you'll find them living in trees. Good news: Big, leafy trees proliferate in Amsterdam's soggy ecosystem. Parakeets have grown accustomed to living among humans, roosting atop the city's buildings. It's not uncommon to be sitting in a cafe and see a parakeet fly by. I suppose this is where lesser travel writers might insert a drug-hallucination quip. But not me!

Lastly, when one hopes to spot birds, remember to look up.

Should they stay or should they go now?

As with any feral population, parakeets have their supporters and detractors. Some people enjoy the cheerful sounds and brights colors of the parrots in Amsterdam. Others say the birds are a nuisance, calling for the city to enact some form of population control. According to DutchNews.nl, the parrots in Amsterdam are considered one of the 10 worst feral species in the world.

Luckily, some middle ground exists between the two sides of the parakeet conflict. Instead of letting the population run rampant or resort to wholesale killing off the birds, researchers are looking to contain or remove the parakeets using humane methods.

Whether people like them or want them out, the parakeets are now an inextricable part of Amsterdam's urban identity. Some say that within years, if the bird population is not destroyed, it will become as ordinary to the city as native birds. Or pigeons are to NYC.

34

Dutch Sauna, If You Dare

No one will ever accuse Europeans, especially northern Europeans, of being shy about their bodies. Even for a body-conscious and relatively conservative American (when it comes to public nudity, anyway!), I admire the European approach to nudity and the human body. They're open and unashamed. Disparate body types are respected. After awhile, it begins to wear off on you. That nude beach you said you'd never dare venture onto? It might just be in your future after all. Ask me how I know.

Unfortunately, prospective nudist, Amsterdam isn't exactly known for its beaches, let alone clothing-optional ones. However, the Dutch, again like their Scandinavian brethren, enjoy a trip to the sauna. In fact, it's ingrained in their culture. There are over 200 public bath houses in the Netherlands alone.

And a trip to the Dutch sauna means going naked.

And co-ed.

Gulp!

A Dutch sauna foray usually consists of shared hot and cold shower areas, warm foot baths, several dry saunas of different temperatures, cold plunge pools, salt scrubbing facilities, a swimming pool and relaxation area, often serving refreshments. You can also rent flip-flops, bathrobes and towels and book a massage.

Don't be intimidated by the co-ed dressing room. Take off your clothes and use a towel or bathrobe to conceal your most-intimate bits when you're moving between areas. Start with a hot and thorough shower followed by a soak in the warm foot bath. Then, cycle through the different saunas with a dip in the plunge pool between each one. Remember to sit on your towel in the saunas, not your naked bum. After a cycle, hit the scrubbing facilities and pools. Each cycle will last about an hour. Complete a cycle or two and you'll be exhausted, ready to rehydrate in the relaxation area. There's simply no better way to rejuvenate and rinse off the urban grime. Plus, you'll sleep the sleep of gods.

And what happens in a Dutch sauna stays in a Dutch sauna. Just kidding! The experience is totally non-sexual. You might even come across whole families at the sauna. Still a little reluctant? Remember, you're a traveler. So, you'll never have to see these people or their fleshy rumps again. Nor they yours.

Give it a go! With decor straight out of 1920s Paris (literally — they stripped an old Parisian department store), the immaculate Sauna Deco stands head and shoulders above the rest.

35

Reinventing the Wharf

erhaps by now you've noticed a trend emerging in my recommendations: I try like hell to balance a destination's major attractions with the proverbial off-the-beaten-path/locals-only tips. Firmly in the latter group, the NDSM Wharf, while pulling in gobs of locals and expats, remains virtually unknown to the international traveler.

Three free ferries depart from the river side of Centraal Station (as opposed to the city center side). Take ferry line 906, the one going to "NDSM-yard." The cruise up the IJ River takes all of 14 minutes, depositing you at this vast, 100-soccer-fields-long complex of entertainment, shopping, eating, office, gallery and workshop buildings.

Until the 1980s, this was one of the world's largest shipyards, regularly launching massive tanker ships. Nowadays, it's a creative colony for artists, artisans, chefs, entrepreneurs and musicians. One weekend a month, Europe's largest flea market inundates the area. There's also a boat that's now a hotel and a long-retired shipyard crane with hotel rooms 30 meters off the deck. And it's home to "cool" companies like MTV and Red

Bull.

Since the ferry's free, come for any reason at all. The flea market. Go shopping. Take a walk. Eat lunch far from the maddening tourist crowd. Check out a music, art or family festival. Or just come to see the reinvention of a wharf.

36

Farmers to Fleas: Thriving Street Markets

Amsterdam street markets run the gamut from high-end and niche to workaday stalwarts stuffed with every product imaginable. While the famous flower market (*Bloemenmarkt*) draws the crowds, these six Amsterdam street markets offer delicious food, interesting bric-a-brac and a far more authentic Amsterdam market-shopping experience than the tourist-touted ones.

1. Albert Cuypmarkt

Amsterdam's Albert Cuyp Market has a rich history of European pushcart merchants and painters. In fact, by the early 20th century, the area had become so congested with these merchants and artisans that the city organized a private weekly market for them to assembly. Since then, Albert Cuyp Market has evolved into the largest outdoor market in Europe. Over 260 stalls of multicultural vendors hawk fresh produce, handmade garments and renowned Dutch Stroopwafels.

Located at Albert Cuypstraat, 1073 BD in the De Pijp region of the Amsterdam's Oud-Zuid district, the market can easily be accessed using Amsterdam's public transportation system. Use the Ceintuurbaan or 2e v.d.Helststraat stations from Tram 12 and 3 and walk a few blocks north. Coming from Tram 4, exit at the Stadhouderskade stop, and the market is a mere 50-meter walk. Trams 16 and 24 will drop you directly at the market via the Albertcuypstraat stop. Visit the market anytime between 9AM and 5PM, Monday through Saturday.

Website

2. Waterlooplein Market

Becoming a day market in 1885, Waterlooplein Square is the oldest flea market in all of Holland. Closed during WWII, the 1950s saw a resurgence in the market's popularity. Nowadays, Waterlooplein Market operates Monday through Saturday, 9:30AM through 6PM. For anything ranging from rare second-hand vintage finds and pristine antique furniture to some of Amsterdam's most delicious edible treats, Waterlooplein Market has you covered. With over 300 stalls open daily, experience Amsterdam's culture at its apex at Waterlooplein Square.

Located just east of Amsterdam's famous Red Light District at Waterlooplein 2, 1011 AL, the market can be easily accessed by foot or by public transportation. Whether you are coming by tram or by metro, hop off at the Waterloo station, and you are steps away from this beautiful historic market.

3. Noordermarkt

Beginning as a pottery market in 1663, Noordermarkt is nearly as old as the Netherlands. Over the years the market has greatly evolved. Today the market hosts a weekly flea market on Mondays (9AM to 2PM) and an organic farmer's market each Saturday (9AM to 3PM). People come in from all over Holland for the Saturday's farmer's market, which features some of the best cheeses, fresh fish and baked goods in all of Holland. The real treat is the market's selection of fresh mushrooms, collected from Dutch forests or imported from Lithuania and France.

Located in Amsterdam's Noorderkerk district (1015 NA Amsterdam), the easiest method of accessing the market on either Monday or Saturday is via tram 3 at Nw. Willemsstraat. The market is a short walk.

4. Amsterdam Book Market at the Spui

The Book Market at the Spui is another unique stop amongst the Amsterdam outdoor markets. As the name suggests, the Book Market at the Spui specializes in vintage and out-of-print books for over 20 years. Offering books in many languages in addition to rare prints and antique pieces, the Spui is one of the most unique of these Amsterdam street markets.

Located at Spui, 1012 KZ in central Amsterdam, you can easily access the book market by tram 1, 2, 4, 5, 9, 16 or 24 or if you prefer, the market is about a 1Km walk from Centraal Station. You'll be able to explore there many books, prints and pamphlets Fridays, year-round, between 10AM and 6PM.

5. Pekmarkt Noord

Founded in 1920 and finding its current home in 2014 at EC, Van der Pekstraat in the Noord Amsterdam district, Pekmarkt Noord has been an Amsterdam street market institution for nearly a century. Located just north of the IJ River, take the tram to Amsterdam Centraal, cross the IJ via ferry (Buiksloterveer) and walk north approximately 250 meters.

Three Amsterdam markets operate out of Pekmarkt Noord. Three days a week (Wednesday, Friday and Saturday) you will find one of the best street markets at Pekmarkt Noord from 9AM to 5PM. Discover a range of merchants offering everything from textiles to local produce. Fridays feature a farmer's market with an emphasis on organic and sustainably produced food. Finally, Saturday's mixed market is one of the most diverse Amsterdam markets. Filled with music, art and a range of local vendors, Pekmarkt's mixed market is a great way to spend a Saturday afternoon.

6. Dappermarkt

One of Amsterdam's busiest outdoor markets, Dappermarkt has been welcoming visitors since 1910. Located at Dapperstraat 1093 BS in Amsterdam's Dapperbuurt district, the market is easily accessible by tram 3, 7, 9, 10 or 14 and is less than a five-minute walk from the Tropenmuseum.

Open Monday through Saturday 9AM to 5PM, Dappermarkt is rife with international culture. It hosts merchants from all over the world, with Moroccan and Turkish influences especially standing out. Whether you are looking for a handmade Moroccan rug or some of Holland's famous tulips, Dappermarkt has you covered.

37

Five for Free

L ow on travel funds? Need a cheap day to balance out the budget? I hear ya. Indeed, traveling Amsterdam puts a pinch on the pocketbook. But good news my friend: Amsterdam also has plenty of free things to do. Here are five awesome ways to save cash without sacrificing experiencing . (And, yes, the cat boat is exactly what it sounds like.)

1. Park it

On a sunny day, go hang out at one of Amsterdam's lovely urban oases. I like Vondelpark and Sarphatipark.

Vondelpark is the big, pulsating green heart of Amsterdam. With four cafes, numerous playgrounds, paddleboat pond, art sculptures — including Picasso's *The Bird* — a rose garden and towering trees home to countless feral parakeets (chapter 33), Vondelpark delights.

Just a couple blocks from recommended Albert Cuypmarkt (chapter 36), Sarphatipark, on the other hand, is small, intimate and caters to a mostly local clientele in the De Pijp neighborhood (chapter 12). On a warm summer day, bring a picnic fetched from the market and watch the world sunbathe/go by.

2. Museum gardens

While all of the following museums charge a hefty admission price, their outdoor gardens remain free and accessible to the public. Take a snack, drink and a good book — you'll be surprised by how quickly you while away a few hours and by how re-energized you feel afterwards.

Artisplein, at the Royal Artis Zoo, boasts beautiful trees, water fountain, flamingo pond and a Dutch polder aviary. Open daily 7AM to 11:30PM.

Though gated, the Rijksmuseum Garden doesn't require a Rijksmuseum *ticket* to enter. The trees provide excellent shade amidst lovingly maintained flower gardens, water fountains and the occasional temporary sculpture exhibition. Open daily 9AM to 6PM.

Okay, while not technically a "garden," this is something far more interesting. Next to the NEMO Science Museum you will find around 20 boats dating from the early 20th century moored and undergoing renovation. Kept under the auspices of the Vereniging Museumhaven (Harbour Museum Society), walk around and browse the informational plaques describing each boat.

3. Cat Boat (Poezenboot). Seriously.

Love cats? Like, *really* love cats? Then, by all means, indulge that love at the Poezenboot, a houseboat sanctuary for stray and abandoned cats. While free, consider leaving a small donation.

Open Mon-Tue and Thu-Sat 1-3PM.

4. Cannabis College

Back to school time! The nonprofit Cannabis College (clearly, the only people in Amsterdam not profiting from the plant) grants information and advice to the public on all aspects of cannabis production and cultivation. You can also tour its basement-level organic pot garden. Open daily 11AM-7PM.

5. Sandwich and a symphony?

Amsterdam's many cultural institutions put on a whole slate of free concerts over lunchtime during the city's self-declared "arts season," which runs from September to June. That said, it's still worth checking the respective websites even if you're in Amsterdam in July or August since these are high-quality productions held in Amsterdam's top venues, an experience usually costing 50 euros-plus.

Muziekgebouw aan 't IJ: Muziekgebouw aan 't IJ, a classical and contemporary music venue on the IJ River, hosts a free monthly concert during the arts season in the main theater on Thursday at 12:30PM.

National Opera and Ballet: The Dutch National Opera and Ballet in Amsterdam holds a free lunchtime concert on Tuesdays at 12:15PM.

Concertgebouw: The famous Royal Concertgebouw holds a free classical concert some Wednesdays at 12:30PM. I recommend collecting your free tickets from the box office the day before.

Westerkerk: An exception to the arts-season rule, the

renaissance-style Westerkerk rocks a noon organ show every Friday between April and October and a free concert played from its 42-bell carillon every Tuesday, also at noon.

38

Festival Fever

Amsterdam has a fever. And, apparently, the only cure is more festival. In fact, the city holds over 300 different festivals every year. (Side note: How the hell does this city get anything done?) Amsterdam's festivals celebrate everything — food, music, gay pride, history, film, dance and plenty more. Here's but a thumbnail of Amsterdam's annual festive gatherings.

Roots Open Air Concert

A well-known world music festival held in Oosterpark every July.

Grachten Festival

The Grachten Festival is a classical music canal festival held in mid-August. The highlight is the free Prinsengracht Concert at the pontoon of the Pulitzer Hotel.

Amsterdam's pen-air film festivals

Amsterdam holds two free open-air film festivals, Pluk-de Nacht (Seize the Night) in mid-August and the West Beach Film Festival in September.

Amsterdam Heritage Days

"*Open Monument dag*" (Amsterdam Heritage Days) goes off in September when about 60 buildings and monuments in Amsterdam and the surrounding area open their doors to the public.

King's Day

King's Day is one of the world's biggest open-air street parties. Held every year on April 27 to celebrate the King's birthday, up to 800,000 visitors cover themselves in orange, cram into Amsterdam and go completely bonkers.

Amsterdam Pride

Amsterdam's world-famous gay cultural event (late July/early August) culminates in the spectacularly outrageous parade on the Prinsengracht canal.

Looking for a festival while you're in town? Check out the tourism website for complete festival listings here.

III

Indulge

Eat and imbibe your way through Amsterdam.

39

Puff, Puff...Pass?

Weed. Herb. Ganja. Buds. The wacky-tobacky (just kidding, no one calls it that). You purchased an Amsterdam book and, therefore, knew this section would be coming.

But before I get into the who, what, where, why and how of smoking pot in Amsterdam, let me first climb aboard my soapbox and state — *hand to God* — **that Amsterdam is one of my favorite cities in the world not because of its tolerance of marijuana but in spite of it**.

There are so many amazing ways to spend time in this rhythmically Nordic city that to spend any significant time in a coffee shop is an utter waste. Wander the great museums, stroll Jordaan's canals, ride ferries to nearby hipster hangouts, bike to Haarlem, but don't get super plastered and stuck to a dingy chair in a smoky room. In sum, don't plan your trip around getting stoned. But I do encourage everyone to sample the city's high life and allow it to punctuate your trip. So, here's the deal with pot in the 'Dam.

First off, as of the writing of this edition in late 2018 and for the foreseeable future, marijuana is not legal in Amsterdam or anywhere else in the Netherlands. It has been decriminalized for personal use...while commercial trade has been largely tolerated to varying degrees and in varying municipalities since the 1970s

Amsterdam and pot...why?

Well, first things first: The Dutch love smoking. Beginning in the Dutch Golden Age (1600s) when merchants began importing tobacco from the 13 Colonies and continuing to today, the Dutch hold a special affinity for social smoking. While lower than their Western European neighbors Germany and France, the Dutch still have a smoking rate hovering around 25% as compared to about 17% in the US and 15% in Canada. In a big city like Amsterdam, that's a noticeable difference.

Additionally, an international trading powerhouse since the aforementioned Dutch Golden Age, Amsterdam has embraced diversity and liberal policies for generations. Amsterdam prides itself on acceptance and cultural freedom. Again, like its fondness for tobacco, this liberalness didn't spring up out of nowhere. The constant influx of immigrants from Dutch colonies coupled with the societal tolerance developed during the Reformation Period, when Amsterdam was a haven for religious heretics, galvanized a social contract based on a foundation of acceptance and tolerance.

So, the table was all set for pot: A liberal, open society that enjoyed a relaxing smoke. It should come as little surprise, then, that when the hippies of the 1960s began smoking weed openly in Amsterdam's parks and streets, the authorities yawned and looked the other way.

And they continue looking the other way. Technically speaking, marijuana sales remain illegal. But, like smoking and possessing pot both of which have been decriminalized (one step short of full legalization) for adults, buying pot (up to 4 grams) is now tolerated and widespread in the city's "green" coffee shops.

Caution: This stuff is potent

This ain't Grandpappy's Thai stick or uncle Herb's Mexican ditch weed. Dutch pot is strong, grown in precise conditions to maximize yield and potency. In this plant's long and storied history, pot has never packed such a punch. The western United States, Canada and Amsterdam have pioneered high-strength flower that routinely exceeds THC-a levels (the plant's active ingredient, which generally predicts potency) of 30-40%. Not all that long ago, only the strongest strains reached the upper teens.

I don't want to scare anyone off, especially regular pot users. Go have a ball. Irregular users, though, should go slow. As the saying goes: puff, puff, pass. And maybe pass again. Sip a sugary drink and let it marinate 30 minutes before toking more. A little goes a long way, particularly if you plan on sightseeing after visiting the coffee shop. Same goes but tenfold for edible marijuana — eat a fraction of that rainbow-colored space cake and wait 30-60 minutes.

What makes Dutch pot so potent? They know exactly what they're doing. Like in the US and Canada, growing pot is a highly lucrative science involving clones, hybrids, LED lights, pot-specific fertilizer blends and scientists with masters degrees in white lab coats. And it's not just marijuana. The Netherlands, despite a noticeable dearth of arable land, is a net *exporter* of food. That's right. Thanks to innovating advanced greenhouse technology, the tiny little Netherlands, that sits on land mostly reclaimed from the North Sea, now grows more food than it needs. Plus, as much marijuana as a continent can handle.

What to expect in a coffee shop

The first thing to expect is a crowd. Amsterdam has closed over half of its coffee shops in the last 20 years. Therefore, the remaining ones invariably draw quite a congregation. I've heard it said that Amsterdam's best coffee shop is the one closest to you. Meaning that all coffee shops sell great weed and the shadiest of establishments have been swept away. So there's little to be gained from hunting down famous or recommended shops. However, nowadays, I'd say that the best coffee shop is the one closest to you *that has space*.

So, like any popular attraction, it's best to go first thing in the morning, which for a coffee shop usually means about 10AM. Other times you might struggle to find a seat. If so, try the bar. Look upstairs. Or ask partially filled tables if they mind accommodating guests; table sharing is common practice throughout Europe and it's no different in a pot shop.

The next thing to expect is smoke. Sometimes lots of it. Pot and tobacco smoke. Many North Americans, and fellow Europeans, have grown accustomed to smokeless bars and coffee shops. Not here. But you came to smoke, right?

Find the pot seller to the side of the main bar or at a separate bar, usually at the back past the main bar. There will often be a menu. If not, ask. Remember: You can look but you can't touch (until you buy). Pot is sold by the gram, usually in pre-weighed bags of 1, 2 and 4 grams. For reference, 1/8 of an ounce equals

3.5 grams. Expect to pay at least €10/gram.

Buy a drink, too. If you're standing at a pot-only side bar, go to the main bar and purchase a drink and/or snack. Technically, it's against the unwritten rules to only buy weed. You're unlikely to find alcohol, but you will turn up real coffee, espresso, bottled sodas and exotic fruit juices (imported from former Dutch colonies).

By far the most common way of smoking weed in Amsterdam's coffee shops is a joint with a 50-50ish mix of tobacco and marijuana. Shops carry papers and blunt rolls at the bar. If you buy pot there, they will usually comp you a pack. Just ask. Pre-rolled joints are also available. Though they represent the mark of a rank amateur, I *suppose* pre-rolls will suffice if your rolling skills aren't up to snuff. Most shops also offer bongs, vaporizers and pipes to rent, borrow or purchase. Again, just ask the "budtender" who will review your options.

If it's your first time and you expect to have a lot of questions, then I strongly recommend choosing a coffee shop somewhere, anywhere outside the old center and Red Light District. Go out to De Pijp (Katsu is delightful) or somewhere west of the Jordaan. Also, patronize your first coffee shop right after it opens for the day. Even if you're not typically the wake-and-bake type. With fewer customers breathing down their necks, staff are more likely to give you, dear inquisitive reader, a thorough rundown of all your consumption options and answer all your pressing ganja queries.

One last tip...

Let it be known, dear reader, that the Original Dampkring is the coffee shop where actors Brad Pitt and Matt Damon were famously photographed after getting super blazed while their non-smoking buddy, *the* George Clooney, waited outside. Also, the interior feels like it came straight off a *Lord of the Rings* set, so there's that too.

40

Get Smart

I n addition to a tolerance of marijuana, Amsterdam also looks the other way when it comes to hallucinogens and soft drugs. And if your trip to Amsterdam involves a mind trip, then you'll want to make a stop at a "smartshop."

What's so smart about it?

Technically, smartshops were named after the herbal stimulants they sell (like powdered guarana) and other products intended to stimulate the mind, improve memory and increase sexual vitality. You can perk up with kola nut, wind down with skullcap or valerian, or stimulate other body zones with aphrodisiacs like muira puama and ginkgo biloba.

But like the good capitalists they are, smartshops have diversified. Nowadays, smartshops sell pot paraphernalia, sex toys, marijuana grow kits, lava lamps (of course) and even souvenirs. However, the main reason travelers patronize smartshops is for the hallucinogens.

Planning a smart trip

Though chemical designer drugs are explicitly forbidden, if it's all natural and hasn't been explicitly outlawed, it's fair game for the smartshops — meaning there are plenty of stronger herbal supplements in addition to the mild ones listed above. Some of the most popular are kratom (a sort of faux-opium), Salvia divinorum (a short-lived but super-intense psychedelic) and cacti (super-strong peyote and derivatives).

Smartshops peddle these light and heavy hallucinogens, often also offering a "chill" lounge for trippers to take their dose. Prior to 2008, there were more than 40 smartshops in Amsterdam, but now there's more like a dozen. After a French tourist famously died from jumping off a bridge while tripping on "magic mushrooms," Amsterdam added mushrooms to its hard drug list. (Side note: Why do the French have to ruin EVERYTHING?!) This effectively banned their sale. Or did it?

Though mushrooms were banned, the authorities never mentioned truffles or infused edibles. The trippy truffles — aka, "philosopher's stones" — are infused with psilocybin (the active ingredient in 'shrooms). So, they are basically the same thing, just slightly watered down. And better tasting.

The experience will last about six hours. Pick a safe, comfortable place where you can hang out for a long time and don't have to worry about acting like a loon. Do it with people you know and trust. Try to enlist at least one sober buddy. Talk to the sellers about what to expect and read all the pamphlets they give you before dosing. And, lastly, make sure you have nothing to do for the rest of the day.

Opened in 1993, Kokopelli smartshop was Amsterdam's first smartshop. It's still operating today, which is a pretty strong testament in Amsterdam's dynamic and quasi-legal world of hallucinogens.

41

A Gratuitous Guide to Gratuity

U nlike the United States, where nearly every establishment seems to have a tipping expectation, tipping
in Amsterdam operates with a different set of norms.
Tipping is not mandatory, but has taken on more of a customary
tone.   Also in contrast to their American counterparts,
hospitality industry workers in Amsterdam receive a fair wage.
Still, if you want to leave tips in Amsterdam, you are certainly
welcome to do so. Here's a quick guide.

Tipping etiquette

Tipping is a simple expression of appreciation for a job well done
as opposed to outsourcing the function of paying the server to
the customer. There are several different ways to leave tips in
Amsterdam. The first is to round up the bill to the nearest euro.
The second way is to leave a few extra coins on the table when
done paying the bill. Finally, the most common tip amount is
10%, left as cash on the table.

Customers should check their bills at a restaurant. Often

times, a service charge appears on the bill, making a tip truly gratuitous. Customers should certainly not feel obligated to tip anything for bad service. You should also keep in mind that, in a restaurant, tips may not necessarily go directly to the servers, but may be pooled together for other restaurant staff.

Outside of the restaurant setting, tipping is not customary in Amsterdam. For example, only tip hotel staff if you're staying at the hotel for a long duration. Tipping of taxi drivers is very rare, except using the round-up method.

Tapped out on tipping? Let's continue.

42

Pannenkoek & Poffertjes

What would Amsterdam be without its beloved batter-and-butter pancake, the *pannenkoek*? Or its smaller but fluffier sibling *poffertjes*? It's like trying to imagine Paris without the baguette, Berlin sans currywurst or London minus fish and chips. Inconceivable!

Thicker than a crepe but noticeably thinner than an American flapjack and larger in diameter than both, *pannenkoek* often come smothered in bacon bits, apple slices, cheese, raisins, simple syrup and powdered sugar. Rather than just a savory breakfast treat, *pannenkoek* are enjoyed as main courses any time of day. Traditionally prepared with buckwheat flour on holidays, *poffertjes* are now eaten year-round. Made in special cast-iron or copper skillets with indentations into which the batter is poured, the Dutch customarily enjoy *poffertjes* as an afternoon or mid-morning snack.

For perfect *pannenkoek* and *poffertjes*, see chapters 47 & 48 for recommendations.

43

French Fries: An Abbreviated Love Story

While the origin of the humble French fry generates much debate (which we'll get to), there's absolutely no denying the fried potato has reached its culinary zenith in Amsterdam (okay, and neighboring Belgium). Golden-brown and thick-cut, Amsterdam French fries are sold on nearly every street corner and come with an array of toppings. I hope you're hungry.

But are they even French?

There is a long-standing dispute over who actually invented fries, with both the French and the Belgians claiming responsibility for their crispy goodness. Some argue vigorously that they should more properly be called "Belgian fries" or "Flemish fries," especially since it appears that the Belgians may have beat the French to frying up strips of potato.

In any case, those who have tried to unravel the origins of crispy fried potatoes generally agree that their popularity skyrocketed during World War I when they were served in copious amounts to all troops, including the British, who ultimately referred to them as "chips," and Americans, who adopted the moniker French fries, much to the Belgians' consternation.

Frieten + Frites

Forget ketchup. Amsterdam French fries come with anything and everything as a topping. You can find massive cones of fries topped with a fried egg and a combination of sauces, but most vendors keep it a bit more simple than that.

Mayonnaise is probably the most popular topping, but that is just the tip of the topping iceberg. Other favorites include curry, peanut sauce, chili, cheese, gravy and garlic sauce, or any combination thereof. Most places charge 50 to 75 cents for each sauce, allowing you to mix and match as you like. *Patate Ooorlog* is a popular French fry dish that features a spicy peanut sauce ("*pindasaus*") layered over mayonnaise and topped with onions. Amsterdam frites are typically served in a paper cone with a fork.

Find the fries

Vleminckx Sausmeesters

Vleminckx Sausmeesters, or sauce masters, is a hole-in-the-wall place that has been serving fries for more than 57 years. All of their fries come prepared by hand and their famously wide selection of sauces boggles the mind. Locals and tourists alike get their fry fix here. Expect a line. But it's worth the wait.

Bar Boca's

Bar Boca's is a sit-down joint so popular that reservations are required. At Boca's you can choose from three different types of potatoes and three different types of sauce. Order all three of each, mix, match and share with friends.

Chipsy King

Haha, I get it. "Chipsy." Whether you need a snack to keep you clubbing, or want to try some of the best *patate oorlog* in town, Chipsy King is the place to go. Located near Centraal Station, Chipsy King is there when you need it, keeping late-night hours.

44

Beyond Pancakes & Fries

Amsterdam cuisine usually elicits thoughts of pancakes and French fries. And that's entirely accurate. Which is why I just devoted two chapters to them. Therefore, it may come as a surprise just how popular, even ubiquitous, Indonesian rice tables are in Amsterdam. Especially if you are unfamiliar with the history linking the two countries.

You see, when Dutch colonists explored the archipelago now known as Indonesia, the way in which Indonesians prepared food and the diversity of cuisine and spices enthralled them. To celebrate this abundance, Indonesian colonials created this elaborate feast called "*rijsttafel.*"

"*Rijsttafel*" is the original Dutch term given to this dining event, translating into "rice table." Although, don't take the name too seriously, as rice is only one of the many components comprising an Indonesian rice table in Amsterdam. This meal entails a buffet of varied Indonesian-style meat, vegetable and fish dishes served in appetizer-sized portions for easy sharing.

What to expect

Over 1,000 islands populate Indonesia, so the cuisine encompasses many wide-ranging styles. That said, all Indonesian cooking is widely recognized for the intention and hard labor they put into preparing food and the freshness and mind-boggling diversity of ingredients.

Generally speaking, anticipate multiple courses consisting of some version of chicken soup with noodles, stewed vegetables, fresh vegetable salad served with a unique dressing, crispy fried fish, grilled fish, grilled chicken, various styles of pork and beef marinated and dressed in an array of sautées. And, of course, plenty of rice.

Traditionally made by hand with a simple mortar and pestle, sweet peanut sauce complements just about everything. But the sauce selection doesn't end there. Other sauces you're sure to encounter include spicy and sweet soy sauces, sweet chili sauce and various curries. Garlic, ginger and onion, along with native spices bold in flavor, make up the base sauces for most dishes.

My recommendation

Of the myriad options, I find myself returning time and again to Tempo Doeloe. With reasonable prices, good service and an easy-going atmosphere, Templo Doeloe continues doing it right.

45

Street Food Valhalla

D o you like the idea of perusing street food from around the world in an atmospheric historic building? How about slaking your thirst with house-brewed craft beer available nowhere else in Amsterdam? Of course you do! Therefore, I do declare, you're going to love Foodhallen Amsterdam.

Foodhallen and De Hallen

Foodhallen Amsterdam is the first of its kind in the Netherlands. The 1902-era De Hallen building where the indoor food market sits reopened in October 2014. A tram depot once upon a time, preservation played a key role during its transformation into a hip, trendy multi-use megaplex. The renovation process painstakingly retained its industrial character while bringing warmth and personalization to each space. The De Hallen Building is packed with shops, a cinema, television studios, apartments, a hotel and galleries. This building is a community unto itself.

The De Hallen's "Foodhallen Amsterdam" follows in the footsteps of other high-concept European street-food markets. Like Copenhagen's Torvehallerne, the Borough Market in London and Mercado de San Miguel in Madrid. Enjoy gastric wonders from 20 different indoor food stalls. From sushi to burgers, dim sum to tacos, you can eat your way around the word without leaving the building. Find your grub, pull up beside some new friends at one of the communal tables and enjoy your feast.

Also, aside from the Foodhallen vendors, sit-down restaurants include Brasserie Halte 3 and Meat West. All three combine to create a hip, trendy and social atmosphere.

Don't forget the libations!

Food isn't the only thing going on in De Hallen Amsterdam. In addition to awesome street food, multiple specialized bars serve cocktails, wine and beer.

First and foremost, there's Beer Bar, offering over 60 local and international beers. They also brew a couple of unique house beers exclusively at Foodhallen. For mixed drinks and wine, try the Wine Bar and G&T Bar, which boast a high variety of gins, tonics, fresh garnishes and wine. The Main Bar includes soft drinks, bottled beer, house wines, mixed drinks and seasonal specials.

46

Bitter Bar Snacks

I f you ever find yourself craving a beer after a day of exploring Amsterdam, make sure to also order some *bittergarnituur*, complete with *bitterballen*.

Come again?

Roughly translated as "appetizers" in Dutch, this assortment of fried finger foods commonly served in bars throughout Amsterdam dominates the bar-snack scene. Delicious *bittergarnituur* snacks encompass a whole range of fried, bite-sized nosh. Find it on the "*borrelhapjes*" (or, "snacks-to-have-with-drinks") menu. No one seems to know particularly when it became a staple of Amsterdam bar snacks. But astute guesses point to its introduction to Dutch cuisine during the Netherlands' Spanish occupation in the 17th century. They are basically croquettes, after all.

And, of course, no conversation about *bittergarnituur* is complete without mentioning *bitterballen*, the real star of Amsterdam bar snacks.

What is bitterballen?

Essentially a deep-fried meatball, often made with gravy baked inside, *bitterballen* rules Amsterdam's cheap food options, the reigning undisputed champion of Amsterdam bar snacks. Traditionally made from beef, veal or a mixture, some creative types nowadays experiment with chicken and fish. Minced or chopped, the meat filling is usually combined with gravy and beef broth. Butter and flour add extra thickness. Furthermore, a dash of salt, pepper and parsley round out the savory flavor profile. If you want to make the most out of your choice, then pair it with a crisp, cold draft beer.

Finding bitterballen

Any place serving alcohol (and even some coffee shops) will likely have *bitterballen* on the menu. But, as with any place, eating in Amsterdam is better some places than others.

BallenBar (inside Foodhallen, Bellamyplein 51, Amsterdam) inside Foodhallen is famous for its "bouillabaisse-ballen," using a filling created by acclaimed, Michelin-starred chef Peter Gast.

Gewaeght Café (Nieuwmarkt 16, 1012 CR Amsterdam) in the popular Nieuwmarkt market square is another fabulous option. Offering the comfortable atmosphere of a traditional pub, complete with great music, the Gewaeght Café whips up an array of classic *bittergarnituur*.

Expect to pay around €5 for a typical plate of 5-6 snacks.

47

Brunch Tough

B runch. It's humanity's gift to itself. Good job human,
you stayed up too late last night and overslept this
morning. Your reward? Gobs of food! Luckily,
Amsterdam eateries — especially the four detailed below —
will happily reward your laziness with a brunch fit for even the
funnest of Sunday Fundays.

Vinnies

Vinnies has two convenient locations in central Amsterdam,
and both are open 7 days a week, 7:30AM during the week, 9AM
on Saturday and 9:30AM on Sunday. This makes both locations
a terrific place to go for an Amsterdam brunch, especially as
they serve breakfast and brunch food all day long. As any self-
respecting brunch establishment should, of course.

In terms of brunch, they have two specialties I love. Their
Omega 3 Breakfast includes a pair of poached eggs on organic toast, along with smoked wild salmon, smoked mackerel
mousse and roasted tomatoes and avocados. They also have a

Veggie Breakfast that includes the same eggs, toast, tomatoes and avocados as well as *baba ganoush* and green-pea hummus.

Locations:

Haarlemmerstraat 46 HS

1013 ES Amsterdam

+31 20 771 3086

Scheldestraat 45BG

1078 GG Amsterdam

+31 20 737 3180

Greenwoods

Like Vinnies, Greenwoods has two convenient locations in central Amsterdam. Also like Greenwoods, they are both open 7 days a week. The one on Singel Street opens every day at 8:30AM, while the Keizersgracht location opens at 9AM. They are the place to go for a hearty English-style Amsterdam breakfast.

One of the things that make Greenwoods special is that they offer a gluten-free vegetarian breakfast. This includes a wide variety of homemade breads, such as their soda bread, that are completely devoid of any and all gluten. I'm still not sure what gluten is, but rest assured these foods have none. If you are really feeling decadent, then try their Banana Bread Tumble. They also offer a big stack of delicious pancakes, and their smoothies are excellent, too.

Locations:

Singel 103

1012 VG Amsterdam

+31 20 623 7071

Keizersgracht 465
1017 DK Amsterdam
+31 20 420 4330

Omelegg

Omelegg is yet another restaurant with two central locations where you can enjoy a terrific brunch, including one in rec-ommended De Pijp (chapter 12). Both locations open daily at 7AM on weekdays and at 8AM on the weekends. Known as the first "omelettery" in the country, Omelegg serves breakfast and brunch all day long.

Like their name implies, omelettes are their specialty. Their Viking Fisherman Omelette includes smoke salmon, and if you are a vegetarian, you should try their Popeye Omelette, which of course includes spinach. They also have a terrific Date Omelette that includes — in addition to dates — walnuts and honey.

Locations:
Ferdinand Bolstraat 143
1072 LH Amsterdam
+31 20 370 1134

Nieuwebrugsteeg 24
1012 AC Amsterdam
+31 20 233 2406

The Pancake Bakery

Overlooking a canal in central Amsterdam, The Pancake Bakery is the place to go for both a great pancake breakfast and a wonderful view. They are open 7 days a week from 9AM until

9:30PM.

As their name implies, the specialty of The Pancake Bakery is pancakes. They offer lots of varieties, too — 18 international-inspired creations, traditional sweet or savory cakes and another two dozen house specialities. That's a lot of pancakes. Here I am, after 37 years of life, thinking that there's only one kind of pancake. Silly me. So, make sure that you go there hungry and consider splitting different pancakes with your friends.

Location:

Prinsengracht 191

1015 DS Amsterdam

+31 20 625 1333

48

Insert Your Own "Munchies" Joke Here

I refuse to lower myself to such low comedic depths and make such an obvious marijuana-munchies joke. But this is where we discuss one of the finer points of eating out in Amsterdam, and Europe in general: dessert time. So, if you have any jokes you'd like to tell yourself in lieu of my refusal, then now is the time.

Done? Okay, great. Let's take a look at three places in Amsterdam sure to satisfy your sweet tooth.

De Laatste Kruimel

De Laatste Kruimel is famous for its cakes *and* pies. You'll want to sit down with a coffee and enjoy your treats because this place is downright adorable. Try their raspberry cheesecake or, my favorite, the zucchini cake with homemade lemon curd. Loyal local patrons cannot seem to get enough of their apple pie.

Hours: Daily from 8AM to 8PM

Location: Langebrugsteeg 4, 1012 GB Amsterdam, De Wallen, Centrum

Metropolitan

Metropolitan specializes in homemade ice cream, gelato and pastries, using fresh dairy milk gathered from across the Netherlands. Sourcing only the very best ingredients, Metropolitan produces a variety of flavors of ice cream and gelato. For example, this shop gets some of their milk from dairy cows on a farm just outside Amsterdam. You can't get any fresher than that.

You'll also find high-quality truffles, chocolate pastries and many other delicious baked goods, using cacao sourced from the Dominican Republic. Only the best at Metropolitan. They also serve a wide variety of espresso-based beverages in a hospital-white environment. And if you just can't get enough, bring some chocolates and pastries onto your next European stop or back home with you. They will pack up your treats to go.

Hours: Daily 9AM to 10PM

Location: Warmoesstraat 135, 1012 JB AMSTERDAM

Winkel 43

Winkel 43 is an Amsterdam classic. Simply put, their apple pie is legendary. You'll find artfully arranged slices all over Instagram. People can't get enough of it and it's easy to see why. When you order your slice of apple pie, make sure you get a house-made cappuccino, too. Enjoy the warm, spicy, apple pie topped with freshly whipped cream. There isn't a better combination around and this pie isn't to be missed. Winkel 43 is particularly adored for its late-night hours, open until 1AM on weekdays and until 3AM on weekends. The shop is a bit small inside but you can take your slice of pie to their patio.

Hours: 7AM/8AM to 1AM/3AM
Location: Noordermarkt 43, 1015 NA Amsterdam

49

Six Amsterdam Breweries (that aren't Heineken or Amstel)

L ike beer? You've come to the right place. Amsterdam is positively awash in breweries. While you've probably heard of Amsterdam's two big brewers — household names Heineken and Amstel — you may not be aware of its burgeoning craft-beer scene, one of Europe's best. Let's remedy that right now.

Amsterdam breweries boasted "microbrewery" status long before that was cool. And the city's added several more high-quality small brewers in just the last few years. Here are a half-dozen Amsterdam breweries I personally vouch for. And I love beer.

1. Brouwerij't IJ

Next to the historic 87-feet tall De Gooyer windmill is an equally historic Amsterdam microbrewery: Brouwerij't IJ. Founded by the musician Kaspar Peterson, this rustic brewery has been serving craft beer since the 1980s.

Using only organic ingredients, Brouwerij't IJ has eight standard beers available year-round as well as three seasonal and a few limited edition brews. Furthermore, you will also find an extensive food menu and a relaxing terrace overlooking a canal.

Brouwerij't IJ's official address is 7 Funenkade in Amsterdam-Oost, which is about a 20-minute walk from the Weesperplein metro station. Open Monday through Sunday from 2-8PM. Take an English guided tour on Fridays, Saturdays or Sundays at 3:30PM.

2. Oedipus Brewing

Founded by a group of friends in 2009, Oedipus Brewing is one of the more colorful Amsterdam microbreweries. This artsy brewery offers 12 unique craft beers, most of which have hints of exotic flavors, on a rotating basis. Some of Oedipus's best-known brews include the citrusy Mama, the spicy Thai Thai and the fruity Polyamorie.

Oedipus Brewing offers different tour and tasting packages (some of which include food) in their taproom. There are also numerous live music events going on throughout the year.

You can find Oedipus' main headquarters at Gedempt Hamerkanaal 85, about a 10-minute walk from the Noorderpark metro stop. Open on Thursdays from 5-10PM, Fridays through Saturdays from 2-11PM and Sundays from 2-10PM.

3. Brouwerij Troost

Although Brouwerij Troost is one of the newer Amsterdam breweries, it's swiftly become one of the most popular. Founded in De Pijp in 2014, Brouwerij Troost now has three new location in Westerpark, Oost and Oud-West. Guests can usually find 12 beers on tap at these locations on a rotating basis. Some of Brouwerij Troost's most famous brews include their light Pilsner, German Weizen and New England I.P.A.

Brouwerij Troost is equally beloved for their food as they are for their beer. The long menu includes exceptional snacks and hearty bar fare including steak, pulled beef tacos, burgers and quesadillas.

Open Monday through Thursday from 4PM to 1AM, on Friday from 4PM to 3AM, on Saturday from 2PM to 3AM, and on Sunday from 2PM to midnight. Brouwerij Troost only offers guided tours at its more spacious De Westergasfabriek location on Saturday at 4PM.

The original De Pijp location is at Cornelis Troostplein 21, conveniently near the De Pijp metro. Brouwerij Troost's West-erpark location is a short walk from the Van L.Stirumstraat bus stop.

4. Brouwerij de Prael

Although it doesn't look like much from the outside, Brouwerij de Prael is a rather large brewery in the heart of Amsterdam. Despite the fact that Brouwerij de Prael is in the steamy De Wallen district, it's one of the best places to get your hands on traditional Amsterdam craft beers.

The 12 drafts on tap at this brewery are based on traditional European recipes and include I.P.A., Weizen and Scotch ale. Additionally, Brouwerij de Prael also offers a few seasonal brews as well as wide range of food including sandwiches, fried eggs, burgers and a kid's menu.

Brouwerij de Prael is open Monday through Wednesday from noon to midnight, on Thursday through Saturday from noon to 1AM, and on Sunday from non to 11PM. You can find this brewery at Oudezijds Armsteeg 26 close to the Nieuwezijds Kolk bus stop.

5. Brouwerij Poesiat & Kater

The Brouwerij Poesiat & Kater has a history dating back to the 1730s. At that time, Jan van den Bosch founded this famous brewery, which became known around the world after future owner Jan Messchert van Vollenhoven created the Extra Stout. Heineken owned this brewery for a time, but in 2006 this historic building was transformed yet again into one of the most iconic Amsterdam microbreweries.

There are between six to nine brews on tap at Brouwerij Poesiat & Kater including the famed Original Extra Stout as well the fruity Falcon Ale and the East Indies Pale Ale. Brouwerij Poesiat & Kater also has a tasting room with specialty beers as well as brunch, lunch, and dinner menus. There are 80 seats in the ground floor area and 40 seats in the mezzanine. Guided tours take place on Saturday at 3PM.

Brouwerij Poesiat & Kater is open on Monday through Sunday from 11AM to 1AM. Located at Polderweg 648, this brewery is a short walk from the Muiderpoort bus stop.

6. Butcher's Tears

Somewhat like Oedipus Brewing, Butcher's Tears is one of the more imaginative Amsterdam breweries offering unique seasonal brews like the Burton ale "Pantagruel" and the barley wine "Old Geezer." In addition to specialty and/or seasonal beers on tap, three year-round Butcher's Tears beers include the Amsterdam pale ale "Green Cap," the amber ale "The Last Possession" and the saison aptly named "Saison en Enfer."

This small, casual brewery often hosts events like movie screenings and live concerts. Also, there's a tasting room at Butcher's Tears where guests can sample fascinating small-batch brews.

Open Wednesday through Sunday 4-9PM, this microbrewery is at 45 Karperweg, Oud-Zuid Amsterdam, a short walk from the Haarl'meerstation.

50

Gin & Tears

The much-heralded VOC Cafe is a bar worth cozying up to, and I do mean cozy. This charmingly Old World Dutch pub is situated in the "Schreierstoren," or Weeping Tower. Once upon a time, when the Dutch East India Company's fleets scoured the globe for rich trade goods and ripe colonial pickings, the wives of these seafaring Dutchmen bid goodbye and kept an ever-watchful eye for their sailors' return home from atop the "Weeping" Tower.

Once an integral part of Amsterdam's 14th-century defensive fortifications, a drink at the VOC Cafe is the quintessential way to experience the Weeping Tower. Sit down and take in the creaky hardwood floors, crusty brown brick walls and the cramped but comfy ambiance of centuries-old Dutch life depicted in artwork and ship memorabilia. Indeed, the VOC Cafe is considered not only Amsterdam's, but also the entire country's oldest bar.

Hours: Daily 10AM to 1/3AM
Location: Prins Hendrikkade 94-95, 1012 AE Amsterdam

51

Hiding in Plain Sight

The HPS-Amsterdam ("Hiding in Plain Sight," for those not in the acronym-know) is one of the Dutch capital's premier drinking establishments. Located in the historic heart of Amsterdam, at Rapenburg 18, HPS-Amsterdam is a small, intimate bar known for its classic styling and unique mixed drinks. The bar is owned by the husband-and-wife duo, Guillermo Gonzalez and Vera Magagnini, who take clear inspiration from the 1920s' Jazz/Speakeasy Era. They pride themselves on the stylish venue and attention to great service. Despite the speakeasy-inspired vibe, the bar does not require any passwords or secret rituals to enter.

The HPS cocktail bar is celebrated for its high quality mixed drinks, as well as the always-changing menu. In fact, each bartender must contribute new recipes regularly. The flexible nature of the menu is one reason to check in regularly, as new drinks are always sliding across the countertop. One of their finest creations is the so-called Walking Dead, a 16-oz rum drink served in a skull glass and set on fire. HPS reaps in international recognition for its overall quality, having been featured as one of the "World's 50 Best Bars" by *The Sunday Times*, the "Best Cocktail Bar in Amsterdam" by *Time Out Magazine* and the "Best Cocktail Bar in the Netherlands" by *Esquire*.

The HPS cocktail bar also serves up well done small plates and boozy brunches for those interested and is especially friendly to the native English-speaking crowd. A word of advice though, HPS is tiny and groups of 4 or should make a reservation.

Hours: Daily 6PM-1/3AM

Location: Rapenburg 18, 1011 TX, Amsterdam

52

A Secret Distillery

Though only open since 2010, Distillery 't Nieuwe Diep has already established itself as a beloved Amsterdam institution. This craft distillery in Amsterdam's far-east Flevopark calls a former pumping station home. (Recall that Amsterdam sits precariously on reclaimed and below-sea-level land.) It churns out roughly 100 different organic varieties of liquor, but specializes in "*jenever*," known as "Dutch gin." Head to the distillery's tasting room, helpfully located right next door, to test out the flavors yourself. Generally, locals have an inclination for sweet *jenever* distilled with apple and strawberry, as opposed to traditionally used juniper. The widely known "*citroen jenever*" also has many devotees.

A day at Distillery 't Nieuwe Diep can feel somewhat like going back in time for a while. Or falling down Alice's rabbit-hole. The scenic, lush setting in green Flevopark enchants you with a majestic feeling like you're a million miles away from the rest of the world. Even though you're still in Amsterdam. Not far from a tram stop, actually. Also, be sure to check out the reconstructed polder pump structure, circa 1880.

The tasting room serves all kinds of general beverages as well. These include coffee, soda, wine and even a Basque-style apple cider. Nosh on meat-and-cheese platters to sop up the booze. The *"ossenworst"* is terrific.

Hours: Like any remarkable "secret" spot, this is the rub. Although it's seasonally dependent, your best bet is from 3-5(winter)/8PM(summer) Wednesday to Sunday. Confirm by phone at +06 50 676 339 and +06 27 076 065 or email at info@nwediep.nl.

Location: Flevopark 13, Amsterdam East

53

Bar Hopping

Amsterdam teems with wonderful watering holes. From old-world cafes to hip taverns, open a tab and linger long at these six destinations. They all offer a great atmosphere, superb service, an outdoor-drinking area and lots and lots of booze.

They may not warrant their own chapters, yet their omission would be a huge loss for the book. And your travels. Hit 'em one at a time for that much-needed post-museum quaff or string all six together for a tram-enabled Amsterdam bar crawl.

1. Cafe de Ceuvel
2. Hannekes Boom
3. Pllek
4. Cafe Belgique
5. Arendsnest
6. Par Hasard

Thirsty yet?

FREE Paris eBook

Receive a FREE Paris ebook today.

After downloading your free book, you'll receive a monthly VIP email with book giveaways, new book announcements and huge book discounts ONLY available exclusively to subscribers.

Join the crew and subscribe for **FREE** to Rory Moulton's monthly email newsletter about European travel, "*EuroExperto*." In addition to the giveaways and discounts, receive the month's best European travel articles, news, tips, trends and more. I'll never spam you. I don't do ads. And you can unsubscribe at any time.

Smarter European travel is just a click away:

www.rorymoulton.com

Please Leave a Review

Did you enjoy this book?

Feel it was a strong value? Are you interested in leaving feedback so that I may improve future editions?

If so, please leave a review on Amazon.

Leaving a review lets Amazon know that people are engaged and interested in this book and will help generate more exposure for it. There are millions of books on Kindle, so your review means a lot to help lift this modest title above the fray.

Thank you!

About the Author

Welcome and thank you for reading 53 Amsterdam Travel Tips! My name's Rory Moulton.

Who am I? I'm a writer, editor, book author and entrepreneur living in the Colorado Rockies with my wife and son. When away from my desk, I'm passionate about travel, woodworking, museums and the great outdoors. And beer. I also really like beer.

When it comes to travel — my passion of passions, and likely the reason you're here — I adamantly advocate for independent, ground-level budget travel. Here are my tenets for satisfying travel:

Focus on experiential — not checklist — travel. Go. See. Do. Make memories. Above all, stay in the moment. Furthermore, Instagram accounts aren't required.

Eat and shop local. Don't seek the tastes and comforts of home. After all, experiencing the strange and new is exactly why we leave home.

Stay in family run hotels and guesthouses, small hostels or neighborhood Airbnbs.

Meet local families. Practice their language.

Picnic in parks, church steps, alpine meadows, cliffside beaches.

Ride overnight trains. Book passage by ferry. Take public transportation.

Sit in the cheap seats.

Eat street food.

See the major cultural sights before or after the crowds. Even if it means getting a little creative.

Avoid glossy tourist traps in all iterations. Be they plastic restaurants, overwrought (and overpriced) attractions or entire destinations.

Plan ahead. However, prepare to chuck the itinerary on a moment's notice when spontaneity calls.

Slow down.

In sum, ditch the all-inclusive, find an affordable flight to a foreign country, fill a carry-on backpack and off you go!

You can connect with me on:

🌐 https://rorymoulton.com

🐦 https://twitter.com/roryam

📘 https://www.facebook.com/EuroExperto/

✎ https://www.instagram.com/rorymoulton/

Subscribe to my newsletter:

✉ http://bit.ly/EuroExperto

CPSIA information can be obtained
at www.ICGtesting.com
Printed in the USA
LVHW090201300419
616058LV00001B/2/P

9 780986 237867